Who Are You, Lord?

GERTRUDE PRIESTER

Illustrated by Shannon Stirnweis

THE COVENANT LIFE CURRICULUM
PUBLISHED BY THE CLC PRESS, RICHMOND, VIRGINIA

THE COVENANT LIFE CURRICULUM
the authorized curriculum of the following denominations:
    Associate Reformed Presbyterian Church
    Cumberland Presbyterian Church
    Moravian Church in America
    Presbyterian Church in the United States
    Reformed Church in America
affiliate denomination:
    The Evangelical Covenant Church of America

The author wishes to acknowledge use of the following translations of the Bible in writing this story: the *Revised Standard Version of the Bible; The New Testament in Modern English* translated by J. B. Phillips; *The Bible, An American Translation,* New Testament translated by Edgar J. Goodspeed; *The New English Bible, New Testament; Good News for Modern Man* (American Bible Society). The author created conversation of characters in the story using these translations as sources. Unless otherwise noted, Scripture quotations are from the *Revised Standard Version of the Bible,* copyrighted 1946 and 1952 by the Division of Christian Education of the National Council of Churches, and used by permission.

© M. E. Bratcher 1969
Printed in the United States of America
First Printing 1969
58-8702

Contents

Chapter	1	At Home in Tarsus	5
Chapter	2	The Adventure Begins	13
Chapter	3	Life in Jerusalem	19
Chapter	4	Trouble from the Nazarenes	27
Chapter	5	Terror in Jerusalem	35
Chapter	6	Jesus Is Lord!	42
Chapter	7	Jesus Is Lord of All Men	50
Chapter	8	Paul Becomes the Leader	60
Chapter	9	Not Gods, but Men!	67
Chapter	10	A Challenge	77
Chapter	11	Come Over and Help Us!	85
Chapter	12	With Friends in Corinth	97
Chapter	13	At Work in Ephesus	107
Chapter	14	To Rome—In Chains	115

Scripture References   127

Dear Reader:

The story in this book is about the apostle Paul. In it he tells us about Jesus Christ. What you will read here is based on what we are told about Paul in the book in the Bible called the Acts. There is much more information about Paul in other books of the New Testament. Almost one fourth of the New Testament is made up of letters that he wrote.

The Bible does not tell us all we would like to know about Paul. We do not know very much about his early life. But we do know how people lived at the time when Paul was growing up in Tarsus. Therefore, we have to imagine some of the things Paul may have done as a boy. The Bible does not tell us what happened to Paul at the end of his life, because no one really knows.

Even though this story is about Paul, the most important person in the story is Jesus Christ. Paul himself tells us that he has been chosen by God to go out and witness that Jesus Christ is Lord over all men. As you read this book, I, with Paul, hope that you will come to know Jesus better.

Sincerely yours,
Gertrude Priester

1
At Home in Tarsus

Saul rolled over on his sleeping mat. He rubbed his eyes and blinked in the bright sunshine. He yawned, and began to stretch. First he stretched one arm, then the other arm. But suddenly Saul remembered something! He sat up and looked down into the courtyard. There was no more time for sleeping today. He had promised to meet his best friend, Demetrius, soon after the sun was up. And the sun was already peeping over the roofs of the houses off toward the east.

Saul jumped up and began to roll up his mat. "I could skip my breakfast," he thought. "But I can't go out before Father says the prayers."

Then the young boy turned to look far, far off into the distance. Sometimes he would pretend that he could hear the trumpets from the temple in Jerusalem far away. Today he closed his eyes and pretended that he was not at home in Tarsus at all. Saul pretended that he was standing right inside the court of that great temple. He began to pray. "Hear, O

Israel: the Lord our God is one Lord; and you shall love the Lord your God with all your heart, and with all your soul, and with all your might." It was the prayer that Saul said every morning, just as soon as he got up.

"I must stop dreaming about Jerusalem," Saul thought when he had finished his prayer. "Demetrius will be coming for me soon. He's not a Jew, so he doesn't have to wait for morning prayers at his house."

Saul ran quickly across the courtyard and inside the house. He went into the room where his mother had just placed some food on the table. There he saw his father dipping water from a jar, and pouring it on his hands just as he did before every meal. Saul watched quietly as his father held up his hands to let the water run down to his wrists.

Saul liked to see his father carrying out the old customs so carefully. "I'm glad we are a good Jewish family," said Saul. "I'm going to obey all the laws when I grow up, just like you, Father."

His father smiled. "You are right, my son. It is a good thing always to obey God's Law."

"Please hurry, Father," begged Saul as the family sat down to eat. "I promised Demetrius that I would meet him early this morning. It's getting late already."

"Be patient, my son. We must thank God first. It is not good to hurry through our prayers. Blessed is he who brings forth food from the earth."

At last everyone had finished eating. Saul squirmed and wiggled his toes as he waited for his father to give thanks after the meal. It seemed like such a long prayer this morning! "It's wrong to want to rush through prayers," thought Saul. "But I don't want Demetrius to go off without me."

As soon as he could, Saul dashed for the door. He stopped just long enough to touch the mezuzah as he ran outside. Demetrius was standing in the shade of the wall, cleaning out a piece of reed to make a whistle. He grinned at Saul and said, "What would happen if you forgot to touch that little box on your doorpost?"

"It's not just a box, it's a mezuzah," snapped Saul. "And I never forget to touch it." Then he frowned. "You wouldn't forget either, if you were a Jew, Demetrius. It's to remind us that God is the one who protects us as we go out and come in. You don't think I could ever forget that, do you?"

Demetrius punched his friend's arm. "I'm only teasing, Saul. You know that." Then he laughed. "The day you forget to touch your mezuzah, I'll give you my prize agate. I know the way you worry over keeping your laws. You'll never forget. Not you, Saul."

"Come on," suggested Saul. "There's a big ship unloading in the harbor. Let's go down and watch the sailors."

The two boys started off down the street. Demetrius stopped suddenly to try his new whistle. "Watch where you're going," growled a man carrying a basketful of figs on his head. "You nearly made me spill my fruit."

Saul had walked on ahead. He wanted to see some slaves writing on papyrus as they sat on mats in front of a book shop. "Come over here, Demetrius," he called. "Here's some good

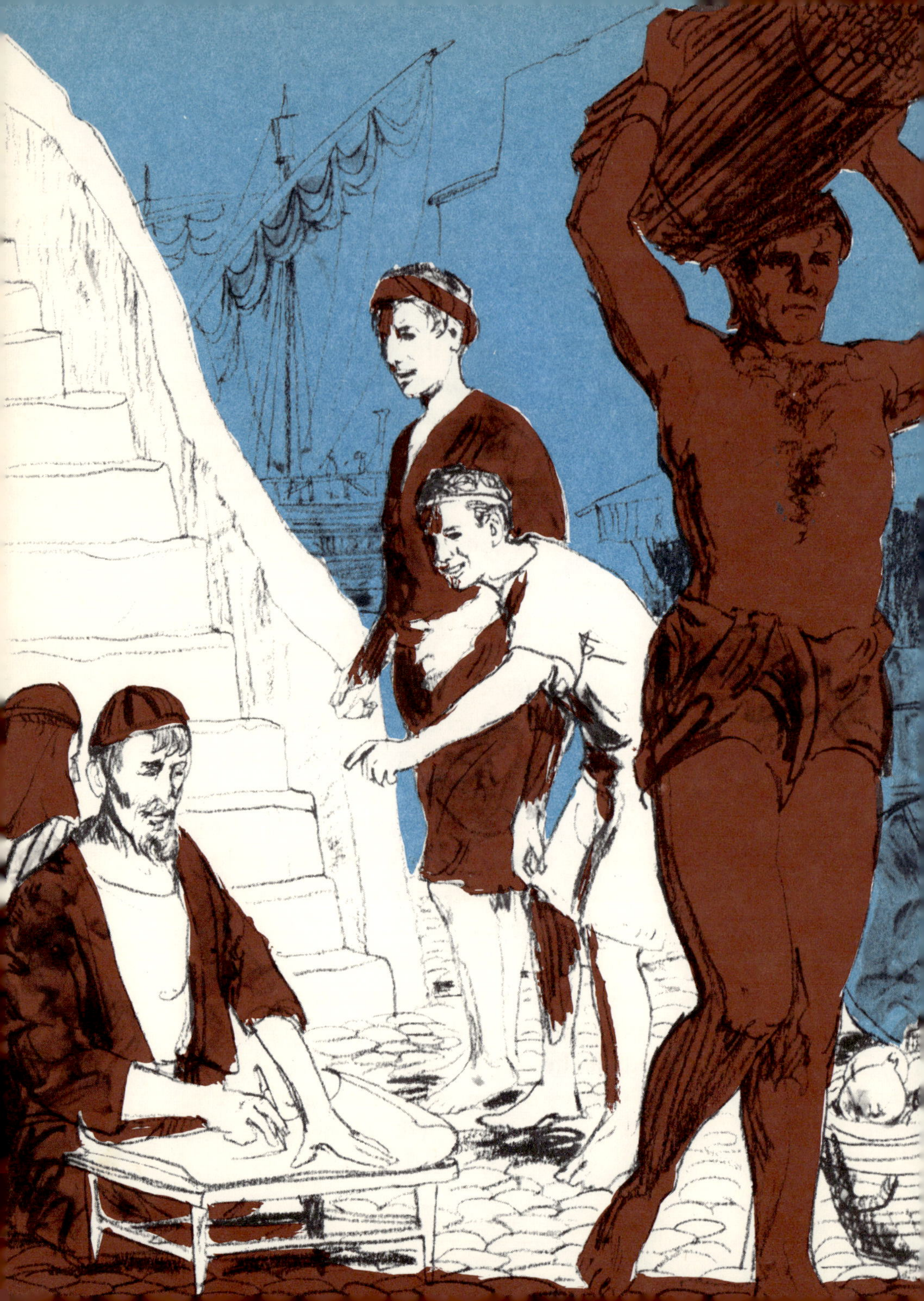

writing for you." Saul pointed to one of the samples the store owner had put out for people to look at so they could choose the one they liked best.

"I like this one," said Demetrius. "It says, 'Life has no blessing like an earnest friend.' A great poet said those words about four hundred years ago. Do you think anyone will remember anything you've said after you have been dead that long, Saul? I'm sure I'll never say anything that important."

The boys laughed and went on toward the river. The streets were crowded with merchants and workmen, soldiers and slaves, and men who lived in faraway lands. They saw a shoemaker carrying a basketful of sandals he wanted to sell. Once they had to jump out of the way of some wagons loaded with grain. They stopped to watch some men sewing canvas into sails for the ships that came to this city of Tarsus from all over the world.

"I've been learning to make tents in old Hilkiah's shop since you've been away, Demetrius," said Saul. "My father sent me there to learn a trade so that I can make my own living. Then I'll always be able to take care of myself, no matter what happens."

The two friends stopped to laugh at a funny old camel loaded with leather for making saddles. Just ahead of them, they saw a man selling spices. He was sitting among his pots and jars. "Ummm. Smell that!" said Demetrius. "I'd rather live here in Tarsus than in any other city in the whole world."

Saul shook his head. "Not me—I want to go to Jerusalem."

"What for?" asked Demetrius looking surprised. "I could understand if you wanted to go to Rome or to Alexandria. But why go to Jerusalem?"

"Because there I can study with our great rabbi, Gamaliel," answered Saul.

"What's so great about him?" asked Demetrius. "We have famous teachers right here in Tarsus. I'd rather stay at home and study here. What's wrong, aren't our teachers good enough for you, Saul?"

Saul looked disgusted. "Gamaliel just happens to be one of the best teachers in the world, that's all," he said. "But you wouldn't understand about going to Jerusalem, Demetrius. You're not a Jew."

"I suppose you'll sit at Gamaliel's feet all day long and argue about your beloved Law," laughed Demetrius. "You'd better be careful or you'll soon know as much as Moses!"

Saul did not laugh. He turned and walked toward a stall where a man was selling figs. Demetrius followed, but he did not tease his friend anymore. It was never safe to tease Saul about his religion, and Demetrius knew that.

"I'm thirsty," said Demetrius. "Let's buy some camel's milk to drink."

"We'll get some of these figs, too," suggested Saul. "We can eat them on the way down to the ship."

The boys wandered along the waterfront and played on the docks. They explored the riverbank and waded in the cold water. Finally they reached the harbor where a big ship was unloading a cargo of grain. There was so much to see and hear and smell!

At last Saul said, "It's time for me to start back. I promised to be home early. We have guests coming to eat the Sabbath feast with us."

"I'm going to stay and watch the sailors," responded Demetrius. "I don't have to get home for any Sabbath feast. But I'll see you tomorrow after the synagogue service, Saul."

As Saul started home alone, he puzzled over something that bothered him more every day. Demetrius was his best friend, but he was not a Jew. His family worshiped the one true God, but they did not keep all the laws of Moses. "How can people like that please God when they are not Jews?" Saul wondered. "Does God really love Demetrius and his family? They do come to the synagogue to worship him, but surely that is not enough! God loves only the Jews who keep every one of his laws."

Saul's mother was getting ready to light the Sabbath lamps as he came into the house. "I like to watch you light the lamps, Mother," said Saul.

"The Sabbath is the best day of the whole week," replied his mother. "It's the sign of God's love toward us forever." Then she covered her eyes with her hands and said the special Sabbath prayer: "Blessed art Thou, O Lord, our God, King of the universe, who hast made us holy by Thy commandments, and commanded us to kindle the Sabbath lights."

Saul watched the bright little flame that must burn all during the Sabbath. No other lamps could be lit, because lighting a lamp was work. And no work like that was allowed in a good Jewish home on the Sabbath.

Then Saul thought about Demetrius, still down among the ships. He felt a little sorry for his friend because there would be no Sabbath feast at his house. Saul felt a little angry, too. He never could understand why Demetrius and his family did not want to keep all the Jewish laws and customs. Everybody should do that. It was the best way of all!

"I'm glad I'm a Jew," muttered Saul as he went to wash himself and get ready for the Sabbath meal. "Just wait until I get to Jerusalem and study with the great Gamaliel. Then I'll learn to be a *really good* Jew."

2
The Adventure Begins

Several years went by before Saul was old enough to go off to Jerusalem. "There is much for you to learn here in Tarsus," said his father. "Rabbi Gamaliel wants you to learn all you can at our own synagogue school before you come to him. Our rabbi will tell us when you are ready to go."

Saul studied hard and learned his lessons easily. Sometimes he helped his friends with the lessons that were hard to understand. "Tell us what you think our lesson means, Saul," they would say. "You always know the right answers."

"I'll tell you all I know about it now," answered Saul. "But someday I will know much more about it."

One Sabbath day Saul and his father were walking home from the synagogue service. "My son," said his father, "Hilkiah tells me that soon you will be able to make tents as well as he can. There is nothing more that he can teach you."

Saul laughed. "The work is easy, Father. My fingers move faster than his. I can make a tent in half the time it takes old Hilkiah."

"Do not speak so about your elders," said Father sternly. "You have learned much from Hilkiah. From now on, you will always be able to earn a living for yourself. But you will not be working with him much longer, my son. I have word that there soon will be a place for you in the school of Gamaliel. Our rabbi says that you are ready now to leave Tarsus and go to Jerusalem to study."

"How soon can I go, Father?" Saul asked eagerly. "I want to learn the laws of Moses more than anything else in the world. I want to know all about how a good Jew must obey them. Then I can please God and win his favor."

"You must begin to get ready so that you can leave as soon as Gamaliel sends word that he will receive his new students," said Father. "While you are waiting, you must spend all your spare time studying the Law and reciting the Scriptures. You don't want the other boys in Jerusalem to know more than you do."

Saul was anxious to tell Demetrius his good news, so he started out to look for him. But Demetrius was nowhere in sight. Just then Saul heard shouts from a playing field nearby. "That's probably where he is," Saul thought. The boys who wanted to enter the foot races to be held in Tarsus during the coming week were timing each other. Demetrius wanted more than anything else to win at least one race this year. He might be practicing with the other boys today.

Saul turned his head so that he would not see the runners as he passed by the field. The games and sports were held in honor of the pagan gods and goddesses, so good Jews never could take part. Saul knew that he would be breaking the

The Adventure Begins

Sabbath law if he even stopped to watch the boys run today. But he had hoped Demetrius might see him as he walked by, and come to join him.

It would not be easy for Saul to leave his family and good friends in Tarsus. But just think of all the great rabbis he would meet! Saul could almost imagine himself being first to answer when the great Gamaliel asked his class questions about the Law. "I will study harder than anyone else," Saul determined. "Someday I may be able to keep every rule and law without breaking one."

The next day Saul was working in Hilkiah's shop. As he sat working on a piece of canvas, Saul was reciting in a low voice: "God is our refuge and strength, a very present help in trouble."

Demetrius came to the doorway. "What are you mumbling about, Saul?" he asked. "I've been standing here for two whole minutes and you never even looked up from that old sail!"

Saul jumped. "Demetrius! I didn't see you. Sit down over there on that pile of canvas while I finish mending this sail. Hilkiah promised to have it ready by nightfall. He said I could mend it faster than he could."

Saul moved closer to the doorway so that he could see his work better. "I have great news, Demetrius!" he exclaimed. "Gamaliel has a place for me in his school at Jerusalem, and I'm going as soon as he sends word that he is ready for his new students. I was just reciting one of the Psalms. I want to be sure I'm ready for the great teacher."

Demetrius looked a little sad. "I'm going to miss you,

Saul. I wish that you could stay here and go to the university with me. My father says that I may study to learn to be a doctor if I promise to work hard. I think it is just as important to try to make sick people well as it is to tell them about God's laws and how to obey them."

"I'm sure you will be a good doctor, Demetrius. And I know that our university is famous. There are some fine teachers here in Tarsus. But I must study with teachers who can help me to know all about God's laws and how to obey them. That's the only way to please God. And that's what I am going to do!"

Demetrius shook his head. "I know you won't change your mind about going to Jerusalem, Saul. Let's not talk about it anymore. Can you come down to the field and watch me run? I have to keep in shape for the big race you know."

"I can come for a little while," said Saul. "I promised

Mother to go to the marketplace and buy some fish. Only a few shops sell the fish that we are allowed to eat. If I'm late, the fish will all be sold."

The two boys walked off together toward the playing field. "I'll come to visit you in Jerusalem, Saul," promised Demetrius. "You can show me all the sights of the city. We can have fun there, too."

A few days later, Saul's family received word from Gamaliel that he was ready for his new students. Saul's father bought passage on a ship that would be sailing from Tarsus in just one week. A good friend, who would be traveling on the same boat, promised to watch out for the boy. "I will see that he reaches Jerusalem safely after our ship docks," he assured Saul's father. "Don't worry."

On the day the ship was to sail, Saul got up very early. His father said some special prayers for a safe journey for all the travelers, and especially for Saul. Then the whole family went with him down to the harbor. The captain of the ship was eager to begin the journey before the good sailing wind could change. He told Saul to bring his bundles on board.

The friend who had promised to look out for Saul was waiting for him. "Let's go up on deck," he said. "We can watch the sailors, and we can see your family on the shore."

Soon the ship began to move. "Good-bye! Good-bye!" Saul shouted. "May God watch over you and keep you safe. Blessed be the name of the Lord."

3
Life in Jerusalem

Saul never would forget the day when he arrived in Jerusalem. The sun was bright and the sky was blue. The golden dome and white marble of the temple sparkled in the sunshine. Even the grim-looking Roman fortress did not seem frightening. He began to recite aloud,

I was glad when they said to me,
"Let us go to the house of the Lord!"
Our feet have been standing within your gates, O
    Jerusalem!

Saul tried to squeeze through the crowd to get a better look at the magnificent temple. Suddenly someone pushed him roughly to the side of the narrow street. As he stumbled against the wall of the nearest house, Saul heard a soldier's angry voice shouting, "Get out of the way, you dogs! Make way for the Roman Tribune."

The boy watched as a company of soldiers, led by their Roman leader, came marching down the street. They pushed people aside, and waved their swords in a threatening way. The one who had pushed Saul continued to yell at anyone who moved too slowly. As he kicked a lame beggar off to the side of the street he shouted, "Get out of the way! Clear the road. Make room for the Emperor's troops!"

Saul clenched his teeth and crowded closer against the wall. "Just you wait!" he muttered angrily. "You don't have to treat people as though they were animals. You just wait until the Messiah comes. He'll teach you Romans who the real ruler is! You won't be able to push the Jews around any longer. Just you wait and see what happens to your mighty army then." When Saul was sure the soldier was not looking his way, he shook his fist at the big stone fortress. Somehow it did look frightening now.

Saul's first days were so busy that he almost forgot to be angry at the Romans. It did not take him long to unpack his belongings and get settled. There were many important things to do. "I must learn my way about the city streets so I can always get to the temple quickly," thought Saul. "I don't want to be late for classes. I also need to find the synagogue where I can go to worship with the Greek-speaking people from Tarsus. I wonder when Gamaliel wants me to come for classes? Where will I find him in the temple?"

Before long Saul knew his way around Jerusalem as well as one who had lived there for years. He explored the temple court. He peeped into the fortress where he saw soldiers playing games on the paving stones of the courtyard. One day he walked to the palaces of the high priest and Herod. He soon learned which of the narrow streets ended up against a wall with no way out!

Saul sent a letter to his father. "This is the greatest city in the whole world," he wrote. "I am going to study hard and learn all I can about the Law. Perhaps I will be a teacher here someday, like Gamaliel."

The first day at school, Gamaliel asked each student to tell why he had come to Jerusalem to study. Saul could hardly wait for his turn to answer. "I want to please God. How can I find out what he wants me to do?" asked Saul.

The teacher smiled. "My son," he said, "people have been trying for many, many years to find the way to please God.

You want to find out too quickly. Sit here with us. We will study the laws together, and think about their meaning. Then we can decide how to be obedient to God. We will learn the Scriptures, and we will study the writings and customs of our forefathers. These will help us to know how to please God. Someday, Saul, you will have both wisdom and understanding."

Gamaliel expected his students to work hard, but he had never had a pupil like Saul. All day long the young man read and memorized the Scriptures. He questioned the meaning of the laws and customs. He tried to understand and obey them all. He was unhappy when he found that he had left some small act undone, even when he had tried very hard to do what was right.

Saul knew that he could never be happy until he learned to keep the Law perfectly. Sometimes he would lie awake at night and try to understand what he had done wrong. "I must try harder to do better," he thought. "There must be a way to find favor with God. Blessed are those whose way is blameless because they live by thy Law, O Lord."

Almost every time Saul went to worship at the Greek-speaking synagogue, he heard news about someone at home. Many of the people there had come from Tarsus. Soon Saul's reputation for talking and arguing wisely and well spread to his home city. His father was pleased, but not very surprised at the reports. "My son has become a leader in the worship of the synagogue in Jerusalem," he would tell his friends.

"Surely there has never been a man of your age who knew

Life in Jerusalem

more about the Law and tried harder to obey it than you," said Saul's fellow students. "You are the kind of son who would make any father proud."

One evening, after Saul had been in Jerusalem for several months, he walked home from the temple tired and unhappy. He had been so busy trying to find a certain scroll he wanted to read that he had forgotten to properly wash his hands according to the ritual. "How will I ever learn to obey all the Law faithfully?" he wondered. "Will I ever feel sure that I am pleasing God?"

As Saul entered his room, he jumped back in surprise. Someone was standing by the little window looking out on the courtyard.

"Demetrius!" shouted Saul. "Where did you come from? I didn't know you were coming to Jerusalem."

The two friends greeted each other warmly. "I couldn't send word that I was coming because I didn't know when I would get passage on a ship," said Demetrius. "I've come to see a money lender for my father, so I can't stay long. But tell me all about yourself, Saul. Do you like being in Jerusalem? Are you learning everything you want to know?"

At first Saul did not answer. Then he said, "Please don't think I'm bragging, Demetrius. But I've gone farther in my studies than many of the students my age. Yet no matter how hard I try, I'm not able to understand every one of the laws and traditions of my fathers."

His friend frowned. "You look tired and unhappy. Are you getting enough sleep, Saul? Do you eat as you should?"

Saul laughed. "You sound just like a doctor, Demetrius. You would think of things like sleeping and eating. But I think that learning the teachings of my religion is more important than taking care of my health. Don't you see that I must become right with God, no matter what else happens to me?"

After Demetrius had gone, Saul sat very still for a long time. He rested his head in his hands. "I love your Law, O Lord. I think about it day and night. I seek your way with my whole heart. Give me understanding so that I may truly keep your commandments. O Lord, hear me crying to you. Help me to know how to please you. Let me know happiness by finding favor in your sight. Blessed is the name of the Lord." Saul was still praying when at last he fell asleep.

Many weeks went by. Saul was one of the group of men called Pharisees. Nothing was more important for them than to study, honor, and obey God's Law. One morning Saul was hurrying faster than usual along the narrow streets leading to the temple. He had promised to meet some of the other Pharisees there, and he did not want to be late.

"Where can all these people be going?" Saul wondered as he pushed his way through the crowd. "Surely they don't believe that story about a crippled beggar being healed by two followers of Jesus yesterday at the temple gate."

As Saul walked along, he listened to what the people were saying. Almost everyone seemed to be talking about those two men, Peter and John, and how they had cured the lame beggar. "Fools!" muttered Saul. "You run after anyone who claims to have magic powers. Men like those disciples of Jesus ought to be punished. That would be the end to their false claims."

When Saul arrived at the temple court, he was surprised to see Peter and John standing before the high priest, who had already begun to question them. "By what power or in what name did you do this?" asked the high priest. "I demand to know how you made a lame man walk."

Saul leaned forward so he could hear every word. "Ignorant fellows!" he muttered under his breath. "They won't dare to speak before these wise men who know God's laws. I suppose they'll swear they never cured the cripple in the name of that dangerous criminal, Jesus. A night in prison will have changed their minds about Jesus being alive. He isn't worth all the trouble he's causing them."

Saul listened carefully as Peter began to speak. "Rulers and Elders, everyone must know that this old beggar is able to stand before you today only because he was healed through the power of Jesus of Nazareth. He is the same Jesus in whom you refused to believe. You put him to death, but God raised him up again to life."

Saul could hardly believe his ears. Healing in the name of Jesus Christ! What a thing to say! Everyone knew about the false claims of that uneducated rabbi from Nazareth. He dared to say that he was the Messiah sent by God! It was a good thing he had been put to death quickly. But these foolish followers of his were still trying to stir up the people with their false teachings.

The high priest and others in the court seemed puzzled and angry. They looked a little afraid, too. The beggar was standing there in front of them, well and strong. Yesterday he had sat outside at the gate, crippled and crying. Out in the street people were praising God for this wonderful work of healing. Saul wondered how Peter and John could be forced to stop saying that they had healed the lame man in the name of Jesus Christ. The crowd would be angry if any harm came to their heroes.

Finally Saul heard the high priest announce the decision. He called Peter and John to listen. "We warn you to stop preaching and teaching in the name of Jesus. This time we will not punish you, but next time we will not be so easy on you. Now get out! And remember—do not speak any more in the name of Jesus."

Saul moved a little closer. He wanted to hear what Peter and John would say to that! Instead of thanking the court, they said, "You must decide which you think is right in God's sight, to obey you or to obey God. As for us, we cannot stop speaking of the things we have seen and heard."

"Those two should have been given a good beating," Saul growled to a man standing near him. "All that talk about Jesus is dangerous. It's blasphemy against God, that's what it is!"

4
Trouble from the Nazarenes

All over Jerusalem Saul heard how Peter and John were still preaching that Jesus was the one sent from God to bring men to himself. "Those men are paying no attention to the high priest's command," said Saul. "We must find some other way to stop them. Every day more people who hear them are joining their group."

One day Saul wrote to his friend Demetrius.

My dear friend,

Some stubborn fellows are causing great trouble here in Jerusalem. They are followers of Jesus, the rabbi from Nazareth, who was put to death a short time ago. They teach and preach about him everywhere. The high priest ordered them to be beaten and put in prison. He even threatened them with death, but still they go on telling about Jesus.

I know what you are thinking, dear Demetrius. What

is one more rabbi with his little group of followers? At home in Tarsus there were many such groups, and everyone believed whatever he liked. But this is different! You should hear these Nazarenes. They preach that Jesus is the Messiah sent from God. Mind you, I'm not saying that they are disobeying any laws. But they believe that loyalty to Jesus is more important than obeying all the laws of Moses. That's one reason why I think they are so dangerous.

I wish you could see some of them, Demetrius. Their leaders are mostly rough men with no education. But when they get up before a crowd and start talking about Jesus, they are like different men. It seems as though something inside them is taking away their stumbling way of talking. They keep saying that God's Spirit gives them power, because it is his will that they tell others about Jesus.

Crowds gather from all over the city to hear them. But you know how people follow a new idea, especially one that says you do not have to worry about obeying the laws! But there is one thing that puzzles me, Demetrius. You know how hard I work learning to keep all the laws. It's no easy job! Remember, you told me I looked as though I was not getting enough sleep? Well, these Nazarenes look so happy about being followers of Jesus. They don't seem to worry about keeping the laws and teachings of our fathers. They do keep the laws, all right. But they are not bothered when they find they have forgotten or broken one.

There is a trap ready to catch one of the worst of them. He's a good-looking young fellow named Stephen. He is very bold, and I admit that he is very clever. Would you believe it, he even preached his lies in my own synagogue? I have debated with him, and I know what a danger he is to our true faith. We are going to stop these men from preaching about Jesus, no matter what we have to do to them. Demetrius, we must always be on the watch for these false gods.

Peace be to you,

                                      Your friend always,
                                      Saul

P.S. I forgot to tell you that Gamaliel surprised us all by advising the high priest to leave these Nazarenes alone! He says their whole idea will disappear if it is just a pack of lies. But if it is from God—well, then we will find ourselves fighting against God. No one is wiser than my beloved teacher. But how can he have doubts in such a matter as this? I am troubled more than I can tell you, Demetrius.

A few days later Saul walked into the temple courtyard. A large crowd had gathered in a porch out of the hot sun. Everyone was listening carefully to a young man who was speaking. Saul found a place in the shade of one of the big stone pillars. He wanted to listen also, for the speaker was the bold, young preacher Stephen. If everything went according to the plan, thought Saul, this would be the *last* time the clever Nazarene preached his false beliefs.

"God cares more about how you think and feel than he does about all the religious laws you obey so carefully," said Stephen.

"Do you mean God does not want us to keep the Law?" shouted a man standing near Saul. "Our fathers, and their fathers, all have taught us that we must obey the Law if we want to win God's blessing."

Stephen smiled. "If your heart is full of hatred at the same time you are obeying the laws, God is not pleased with you," he answered. "Jesus shows us this new way of life for all men. It is for all you who are listening to me, no matter who you are."

Suddenly there was a noise and some scuffling at the edge of the crowd. "I don't want any new way that says I can break God's laws!" one man argued. He began to push toward Stephen.

"Nor me! Nor me!" shouted several others, who also rushed toward the young preacher.

All at once Saul saw that Stephen was being surrounded by a group of strong men. They began to push and pull him toward the hall where the council of religious leaders was meeting. Almost before he knew what had happened, Stephen was standing before the elders listening to the charges being made against him.

Saul would have been surprised if he had known what Stephen was thinking. "I knew this would happen to me one day," thought Stephen as he looked around the room. "These men hate me. They even have the power to kill me. But somehow I am not afraid. God is with me."

Saul found a place in the crowded room where he could once again listen to Stephen. "We'll see what he says now," muttered Saul to himself. "He won't stand there looking so happy about everything much longer."

The witnesses began to make their charges. "He says Jesus of Nazareth will tear down our temple," said one angry man.

"He talks against our holy laws," charged another. "He says Jesus will change the customs Moses gave to our forefathers."

Saul watched as Stephen listened quietly. The young man seemed to be talking to himself. Saul leaned forward, but he could not hear what Stephen was saying. "I know Jesus is with me. Whatever happens, he will never leave me," said Stephen to himself. "I know it is God's will that I tell the good news that Jesus lives!"

The high priest was speaking. "Is what these men are saying about you true?"

Stephen looked around the room once again. "My brothers and fathers, hear me," he began politely. "I ask you to remember that when our nation began long, long ago, God did not speak to our forefather Abraham here in Jerusalem. God did not give Moses the Law here in this temple. There is no one special place where God is to be found. He does not live in man-made houses. The prophets told you this. Everything in heaven and on earth belongs to God, for did he not make them?"

"He's clever," thought Saul. "I have to give him credit for that. He's brave, too. I wonder if I could look as calm as he does if I were on trial for my life? He seems to have forgotten that he is our prisoner."

Stephen went on talking. "You are just like your fathers; you fight against the Spirit of God. You persecute his prophets. You even killed the one whom God sent to you. You have received God's Law, but you do not keep it."

The council members jumped to their feet with angry shouts. Some were so enraged they could not speak, but could only grind their teeth at Stephen to show their feelings.

"Kill the blasphemer! He's a traitor!" they shouted.

In the midst of the noise and confusion, Saul watched Stephen calmly looking out over the heads of the angry men.

He could just barely hear Stephen say, "The heavens have opened. I see Jesus standing at the right hand of God."

Then Saul saw the angry men rush toward Stephen. They dragged him out of the room and hurried with him across the courtyard of the temple. They pushed him down the narrow streets, sending donkeys and people scattering out of their way. At the top of a stoney hill just outside the city, they flung Stephen down into a shallow pit. Quickly the men began to gather a supply of rocks. Those who had spoken against Stephen stripped off their coats. Saul pushed his way to the edge of the crowd. Some of the men threw their coats at his feet for safekeeping.

"Hurry and get on with the stoning of this fellow," growled Saul. "There are more like him who must be destroyed. Throw your rocks. Get it over with!"

Saul watched as the sharp-edged stones cut into Stephen's skin. The heavy rocks beat him to the ground. The pain was terrible to see. "Why doesn't he cry out?" Saul wondered.

Then a strange thing happened. As Saul watched, it seemed as though Stephen's face began to glow with happiness. "Lord, receive my spirit!" he cried. And as the heavy stones beat him down for the last time, he called out, "Lord, do not hold this sin against these men." Stephen lay quiet and still. He was dead.

Saul turned away quickly. He felt angry and puzzled. Now he was more determined than ever to get on with the fight for God. "That's one Nazarene who won't tell lies anymore," he mumbled as he looked back at Stephen's body. "We'll hunt the rest of them down, too. We're not going to stand by any longer and let them threaten to destroy the temple and God's holy Law."

5
Terror in Jerusalem

Saul carried out his threat. Soon all the Nazarenes in Jerusalem knew that he was hunting them.

One night a few weeks later a little group of people sat huddled together in a dark room of a house in the city. "We must decide tonight whether we dare stay here in Jerusalem any longer," whispered one of the men. "Today the high priest's men broke into my neighbor's house. They took his whole family off to prison."

Another man spoke. "When my brother refused to say that Jesus is not alive, Saul's men dragged him out into the street and beat him. They went off and left him lying there. They said they wanted to teach the rest of Jesus' followers a lesson."

"Saul—just the sound of his name scares me!" said another. "He's after us night and day. He says he won't stop until he has killed every one of us, or driven us out of Jerusalem. I think that murderer knows every street and alley in this city!"

"Listen carefully, then," said the first man. "You remember how Nathan and some of our other brothers in Christ escaped from the city a few weeks ago. They got away in the middle of the night."

"They hid in the stadium while Saul's men were smashing up their houses," said someone. "When he arrived and found that they had escaped him, he acted like a madman."

The first speaker continued, "I have word that our friends are now living safely in Damascus. They want us to join them there. Here's my plan for our escape."

The people talked far into the night. "Now let us thank God for Jesus Christ who is not dead but alive! He will be with us, no matter what happens. Even death will not take us away from him. Blessed be God who has given us Jesus. Amen."

On that same night, in another room in Jerusalem, Saul tossed and turned on his bed. "How tired I am," he thought. "I must get some rest before I start out on that long trip tomorrow. Those stubborn followers of Jesus! They think they have escaped me by going off to Damascus and other cities where they can spread their talk about Jesus. God's work must be done. They must be stopped, and I am going to stop them!"

Saul got up and began to walk back and forth across his room. "I have had those people beaten and tortured and thrown into prison cells. They should be screaming and cursing at me. Instead they call on God to forgive me! I can't be doing wrong when I am doing God's work, can I? They act as though they really believe that Jesus is still with them." Saul kicked at his mat. "I'll stamp out this business once and for all. There won't be a Nazarene left in Jerusalem or Damascus or anywhere else when I get finished. But now I must get some sleep."

At daybreak Saul and a company of men set out on the long journey to Damascus. He felt his pouch to be sure he had the letter giving him permission to hunt out the followers of Jesus in that city and send them to prison. "I wish Damascus were not so far away," said Saul to one of his companions. "I am eager to get on with this work for God."

At first the other man was silent. "I wonder why the great Gamaliel said we should leave these Nazarenes alone," he said. "That puzzles me."

Saul's eyes blazed with anger. "Gamaliel is too cautious. Anyway, he said their way would fail if it was all their own idea. We know it's nothing more than that. It certainly is *not* God's way! Let's ride on faster."

Saul and his men rode for hours in the hot sun along the dusty road. "Why did Gamaliel advise us to leave these followers alone?" he wondered. "If their plan is God's will, then I am fighting God. That can't be! No one tries harder than I do to fight *for* God. But how can the Nazarenes go on telling everyone that Jesus is the one sent from God, no matter how many of them I drag off to prison? What makes them so sure? More and more people seem to believe them, no matter what I do to prevent it."

Saul counted all the fishing boats he could see out on the

Sea of Galilee. He recited the writings of one of the prophets. He carefully figured out how far it was to the next town. Saul did everything he could think of to keep from remembering Stephen and his strange words: "Lord, do not hold this sin against these men." But the words haunted him.

The trip to Damascus took several days. The sun was very hot, and all the men grew weary. Every time the company stopped to rest, Saul was the first to be ready to ride on again. He could hardly wait to get to Damascus to start his search.

Everyone was glad to hear one of the group announce, "Damascus is not far off, now. Since it is almost midday, I think we should stop to eat and to rest. We can reach the city easily by nightfall."

Before anyone could answer, a strange thing happened. A light flashed from the sky, and Saul fell to the ground. He heard a voice saying, "Saul, Saul, why do you persecute me?"

"Who are you, Lord?" asked Saul.

The voice answered, "I am Jesus, whom you are persecuting. Get up now, and go into the city. You will be told what you must do."

The men with Saul were speechless. They looked around to see who had spoken, but they could see no one. Saul got up from the ground and began to grope around like a blind man. Horrified, the men exclaimed, "He can't see! He's blind! We must find someone to take care of him." So they took Saul by the hand and led him down the road toward the city.

For three days Saul sat alone in the house of a friend in Damascus. He refused to eat or to drink anything. He did not

Terror in Jerusalem 39

want to talk to anyone. "I cannot see with my eyes," he thought, "but I see many things in my mind. I worked hard to know and obey God's law so that he would be pleased with me. But my way was all wrong! Now Jesus has shown me that God's love is a free gift. I did a terrible wrong to the followers of Jesus. How they must despise me! Now I want to be one of them. I know that Jesus is alive. But will anyone believe I've changed? O Lord, what shall I do? What can I do?"

Saul tossed about on his mat. He thought about the followers of Jesus who lived in Damascus. Would any of them dare to come to him? Or would they be frightened and hide when they found out that he was in the city?

Then it seemed to Saul that he was dreaming about someone coming to restore his sight. It was not a dream! It was real. He felt a hand on his head. Saul heard a voice saying, "Brother Saul, the Lord Jesus who appeared to you on your way here has sent me to you so that you may see again and be filled with God's Spirit."

Saul opened his eyes. He could see! Ananias, a disciple from Damascus, was standing there. The man spoke again in a quiet voice. "Brother Saul, the Lord has sent me to tell you that he has chosen you to be a witness for him to all people. You are to tell what you have seen and heard, both to the Jews and to those who are not Jews. The Lord will show you what you must do."

At first Saul could scarcely speak. This man Ananias was one of the very people he had come here to arrest. But Ananias had just called him "Brother Saul."

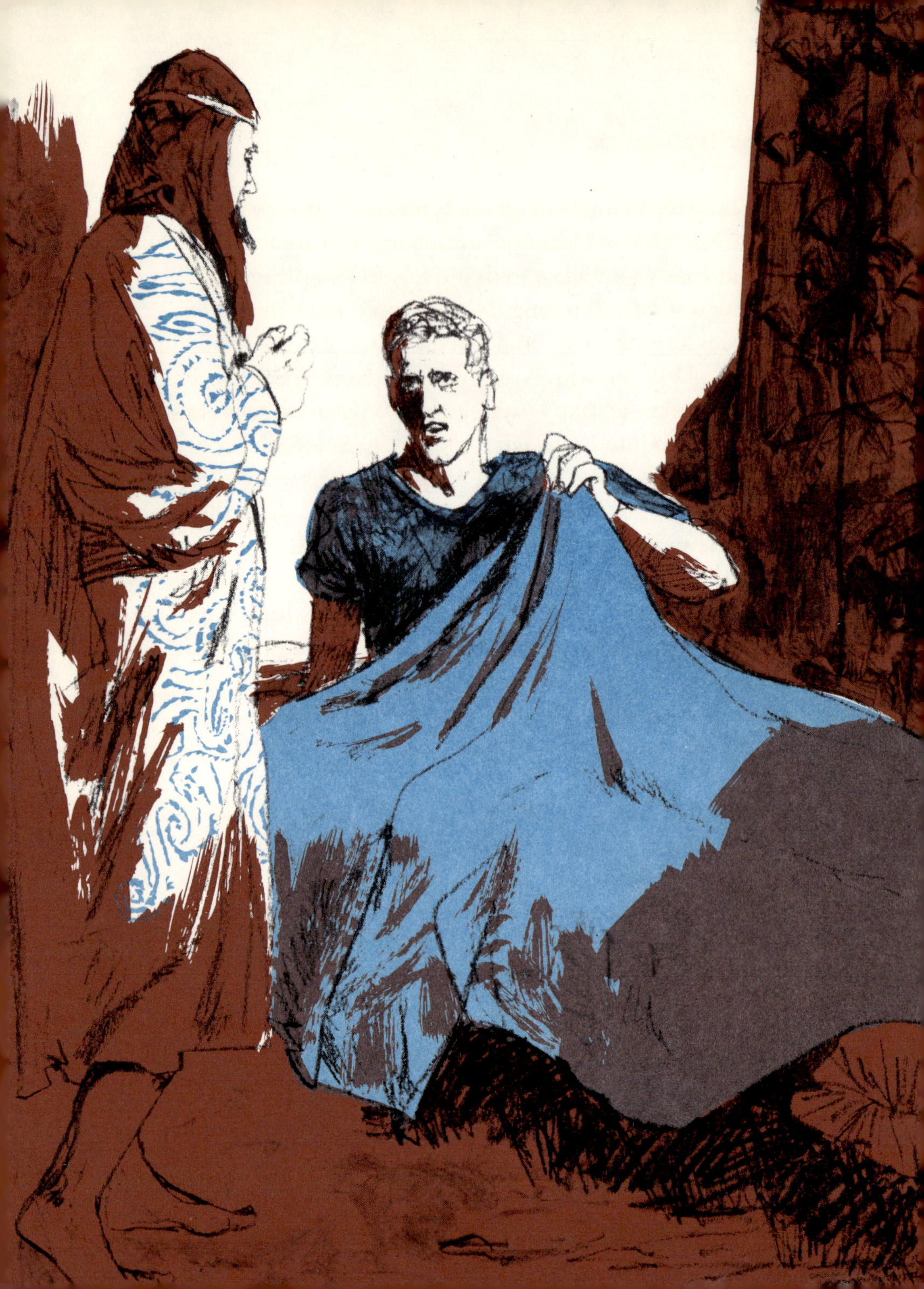

"He does not hate me. Ananias accepts me," thought Saul. "He risked his life by daring to come here. He has forgiven me for what I meant to do to him. Now he tells me that I am to be a witness for Jesus Christ, in spite of all the wrong I've done."

Ananias was speaking again. "Brother Saul, the sign by which we followers of Jesus make known what we believe is baptism. Will you join us in the fellowship and be baptized?" Saul agreed gladly.

"I am baptized in the name of Jesus Christ," said Saul when the service had ended. "Why didn't I see earlier that Jesus is God's Messiah? O Lord, I must undo some of the wrong I have done to you! I will spend my whole life telling men of your great love. I will even go to the ends of the earth if you send me. There is nothing I want more than to tell others that Jesus is Lord!"

6
Jesus Is Lord!

Saul could hardly wait to tell others what had happened to him. "Jesus is alive! He came to me and spoke to me. God's own Son has come to all men. Once I hated him, but he loved me. I was fighting against him, but he has forgiven me. God's love and forgiveness are free to anyone who will accept them."

Everything that Saul had believed about Jesus until now was changed. He had worked hard to do what was right so he could win God's favor. "Now that I have seen Jesus," said Saul, "the way I think and the way I want to act are different. I need to go off by myself for a while. I am not ready to tell others about Jesus until I understand a little better what has happened to me."

Saul left his new friends in Damascus and went away by himself for a while. He wanted to pray and get ready to preach the good news about Jesus.

One day in Damascus a group of Nazarenes sat eating together. A young man burst into the room. He was so out of breath he could scarcely speak. "Brothers!" he gasped. "I have just come from the synagogue. Who do you think is preaching there?"

The others were startled. "You must have run all the way," someone said. "Who is preaching who could cause so much excitement? Tell us!"

"It's Saul! That man who came here from Jerusalem not long ago. Remember him? He meant to put us in prison and destroy our faith," said the young man. "I think it's a trick of some kind. I ran to warn you."

"It could be a trick, but what's Saul saying?" asked one of the men. "He does have a right to speak in our synagogue if he wants to."

"But you know what he did—and now he's saying right out in public that he believes Jesus is God's own Son. I heard him myself!" argued the young man.

Another man spoke up. "I think Saul really believes in Jesus; he means every word he is preaching. I know that's hard to believe. We all remember how frightened we were when he first came here. We expected nothing but trouble from him. But I ask you to wait for a while and see what happens when his old friends hear him preaching about Jesus. Saul will be in the same kind of trouble he meant to cause us. That will be the time for him to prove that he really is one of us."

Saul was a powerful preacher. Soon people from all over Damascus were coming to listen to him. His enemies began to plot against him. "That turncoat! How can he stand there and preach that Jesus is God's Son? He came here to send

Jesus' followers to prison. Now he claims he is one of them. He's saying that Jesus is King of the Jews. That's treason. We ought to arrest him. The king's men will help us get rid of this scoundrel."

By this time there were people in Damascus who believed in Saul and trusted him. They learned of a plot to kill Saul, and planned how to save him. One dark night his friends led him to a house built right into the city wall. "Guards are posted at all the gates day and night," they told Saul. "But we think we can get you to safety without being seen. We will lower you outside the wall in this big basket."

"I don't want to leave you," said Saul. "You are the first to believe that I am a changed man."

"We'll miss you, Brother Saul, but we will all be in danger if you stay any longer. Now we are allowed to meet quietly in our homes and worship in the synagogue. If you stay here and preach publicly that Jesus is Lord, the Jews will begin to persecute us the same way you meant to do when you came here. There are other places where you can preach without causing so much trouble."

Saul knew that his friends were right. At last he said goodbye and climbed into the big basket. Someone fastened the lid so that Saul could raise it easily from the inside. Then they carefully fastened ropes to the basket and let it out the window. Down, down, down the outside of the wall it went. Then ... bump! The basket sat safely on the ground outside the city wall.

Saul stayed very still to be sure none of the guards had seen anything suspicious. Then he raised the lid and peered out . . . all clear. Saul climbed out of the basket and looked around, thinking, "I'm glad it's a dark night. The guards won't be able to find me even if they do discover the basket. I'll keep close to the shadow of the wall until I reach the road."

Saul crept along the wall, listening carefully for anyone who might be following him. All he heard were some little animals scurrying back into their holes. Soon he reached the roadway where he knew he was safe from the guards. He began running down the dark, lonely road leading to Jerusalem. "I must get as far as I can before the sun comes up," he thought.

Trouble began almost as soon as Saul arrived in Jerusalem. "Saul is back here pretending to be a follower of Jesus," one of the disciples reported. "He says he has seen the Lord and has come to preach in his name. I don't believe him."

"It's a trick," said others. "Remember how he hunted us down and tried to stop us from preaching? I say we should have nothing to do with him. Send him away. He can only cause trouble. How do we know he has seen Jesus?"

A man named Barnabas rose to speak. "Listen while I tell you what has happened to Saul since you last saw him. I'm sure you remember that he started out for Damascus to hunt down and arrest the believers there. But before he reached the city, our Lord himself came to Saul on the road and spoke to him. Saul has been a changed man ever since he met Jesus. Recently in Damascus he has been preaching so boldly in Jesus' name that his enemies tried to kill him. Our brothers there helped him to escape from the city, so there would not be any more trouble for the fellowship. Now he has come to us and we must take him in."

Finally the leaders, Peter and James, agreed to allow Saul to meet with them. He told them his strange story about meeting Jesus on the Damascus road. "I thought I was right in acting as I did to persecute you," he explained. "I thought I was pleasing God by fighting to keep the faith free from ideas like yours—I mean ideas like *ours* now! But I was wrong. I know that Jesus is Lord, and I want to preach in his name. You must believe me!"

The disciples believed what Saul said, and accepted him

as one of the followers of Jesus. Soon he was busy preaching in the synagogue, or any place where he could find people who would listen. "Saul is keener than ever," said one of his old friends. "I warn you not to get into an argument with him now or you may find yourself becoming a follower of Jesus before you know it! He sounds so sure of himself. It's not hard to believe what he is preaching and teaching about Jesus."

The Jewish leaders in the temple were furious. They warned Saul to stop preaching in Jesus' name. They threatened to kill him if he disobeyed. "I will never obey such a command," Saul assured the other disciples.

"If you stay here, the persecution may begin all over again and you may be killed," they said. "We all may be put in prison and there will be no one to help us. The high priest is already angry. We must get you out of Jerusalem while there is still time."

"What does God want me to do?" Saul wondered. "Does he want me to stay here and go on preaching?"

One day Saul was praying in the temple. He heard the Lord saying to him, "Hurry and leave Jerusalem quickly. The people here will not believe what you say about me. I will send you far away to preach to those who are not Jews."

Once again Saul said good-bye to his friends and prepared to leave Jerusalem. "I am going home to Tarsus," he said. "The Lord has chosen me to preach in his name. I will wait there until he shows me what I must do."

Rome

MACEDONIA

Philippi

Corinth

MEDITER

BLACK SEA

- Antioch
- Ephesus
- Lystra
- Tarsus
- Antioch
- Cyprus
- Paphos
- MEDITERRANEAN SEA
- Damascus
- Nazareth
- Sea of Galilee
- Jerusalem

7
Jesus Is Lord of All Men

"Saul! Saul! Open the door! It's Barnabas." A man stood in the street knocking at the door of Saul's house in Tarsus.

"Barnabas, how glad I am to see you!" said Saul. "What are you doing here? Where have you come from? Come into the courtyard and tell me how the work is going. How are the other disciples? Here is some water to wash your feet."

"Wait a minute," laughed Barnabas. "One question at a time. I have much to tell you, so let's sit down and talk."

"It's cool here in the shade," said Saul leading his friend toward a stone bench. "Tell me, Barnabas, what's happening in Jerusalem?"

"There has been some trouble among the brothers there," answered Barnabas. "Peter says that we should welcome non-Jews into the fellowship. He tells us we're wrong to insist that they must follow all the Jewish customs and obey the laws of Moses. Peter even eats at the same table with Gentiles, and visits in their homes. You know our strict rules about eating with people who are not Jews, Saul. So you can imagine how some of the disciples feel about all this."

"How do you feel about it, Barnabas?" asked Saul.

"I'm with Peter in this matter," replied Barnabas. "I believe we should welcome all who believe in Jesus and want to follow his way."

"You're right, Jesus Christ is for all men." Saul began to pace about the court as he talked. "Whoever calls on his name will be saved. There is no reason to make a difference between Jews and non-Jews. There is one Lord who is Lord of all!"

"You don't have to preach to me," quipped Barnabas with a smile. "I already believe all that. Let me tell you why I've come to talk to you, Saul. You and I have grown up among the Greeks, and we have always had many non-Jewish friends. It's easier for us to welcome them into our fellowship than it is for others who have known only Jews for most of their lives. Therefore, we must have patience with our brothers who do not see this matter as we do. We can't waste our time arguing about it with them."

"But what can we do?" interrupted Saul. "We can't sit back and keep quiet! We cannot allow our brothers to keep certain people from knowing Jesus just because they're not Jews."

"I've just come from Antioch," continued Barnabas. "There I found many believers who had escaped from Jerusalem at the time of the persecution. I don't need to remind you of that, Saul. They've been preaching to the non-Jews in Antioch very successfully, and have asked me to find someone to help in the work there. I want you to come with me to Antioch, Saul. The Gentiles there are waiting to hear about Jesus, and no one is better fitted to preach to them than you. I'm sure many will become believers as soon as they hear the good news. This will be better proof that any argument that non-Jews can be as true disciples as Jews are."

Saul thought for a moment. "I'll be glad to go back to Antioch with you. We'll preach Jesus Christ to everyone who will listen. This surely is what God wants us to do."

A short time later Saul and Barnabas arrived in Antioch.

"There is a new preacher in our city," said the people. "His name is Saul. He preaches that Jesus is Lord of all of us, not just of the Jews."

"Oh, he's one of those 'Christ-men,'" said someone. "I went to one of their meetings not long ago. They all seem so happy, it makes me want to know more about their Jesus. If they're right about him, perhaps I shall join their fellowship. I'm not a Jew, but they said I was welcome anyway."

One day Barnabas told Saul that a teacher named Agabus had just arrived from Jerusalem. "He brings bad news," said Barnabas. "Agabus reports that our brothers are once again being hunted down and put into prison. Worst of all, he says that a time of famine is near when there won't be enough food for all the people in Jerusalem. You know what that will mean for our friends, Saul. They'll have to stay in hiding and might starve to death. We must find a way to help them."

Saul immediately told the believers in Antioch what was happening to their brothers in Jerusalem. "We are all part of the same fellowship in Christ," said the people. "Let's collect money and send it to our Jewish friends who are in need. They can buy food and whatever they must have while the famine lasts. We'll show them that because of the faith we all have in Jesus Christ we want to share the troubles that have come to them."

As soon as the money was collected, Saul and Barnabas were chosen to carry it safely to Jerusalem. "May God bless your people for this gift," said the elders who received the money. "The Emperor Claudius tells us that food will continue to be scarce and very costly. Now we can buy enough so that our families will not die of hunger. We are glad to know that you care about us and want to share in our troubles."

"We are called Christians now," said Barnabas with a smile, "because we preach Christ everywhere we go. The nickname 'Christ-men' or 'Christian' has become the name that everyone calls us. We're proud of it. Perhaps people will begin to call you Christians, too. Saul and I bring to the Christians in Jerusalem a gift from their brother Christians in Antioch."

Saul and Barnabas returned to Antioch. A year passed, and the church there was growing stronger. Many good leaders began to take over much of the work. One day all the people met to pray together about sending Saul and Barnabas out to preach the good news to those who had not had a chance to hear about Jesus. "We have received the good news, and we must be sure that others hear it, too," they decided. "Grant, O Lord, that Barnabas and Saul may go out to speak boldly, so that the news of Christ may be spread in faraway places."

"Let's take my young cousin Mark with us," said Barnabas. "He can learn something from a preaching trip like ours. Perhaps he may be able to help, too."

Soon afterwards, the three men said good-bye to their friends in Antioch. They sailed off to the island of Cyprus, where Barnabas had been born. He was excited over the chance to see some of his old friends. Saul was excited because he knew he would find people who had never heard about Jesus. Mark was excited because he loved to travel, he was fond of his cousin Barnabas, and something was sure to happen whenever a man like Saul was around.

"Barnabas, welcome back!" The travelers were greeted by many friends of Barnabas during their first days on the island. "Do you bring us new teachings? Come speak in our synagogues."

Saul found that there were some people in Cyprus who had heard of Jesus in earlier days. Those who believed in him were eager to know more. Some who had never heard the story listened curiously at first. Then many of them believed also. The people were overjoyed to learn that God's love was for all men. They were especially glad to hear that faith in God through Jesus Christ was the way to a new life, and that they did not have to keep countless Jewish laws and customs.

Day after day the preachers traveled about the island. They spent most of their time teaching and preaching in the synagogues, and visiting in the homes of friends or fellow-believers. One day in Paphos, the city where the Roman Governor lived, the men preached in the marketplace. That evening they were resting in the coolness of the courtyard when they heard a knock at the door.

"I am looking for the men who preached in the marketplace today," said the stranger whom Barnabas found standing at the door. "My master, the Governor, wants them to come to him tomorrow at midday. He wants to hear what they were saying."

"You have come to the right house, for we are the men who spoke today," said Barnabas.

Saul was looking over his friend's shoulder. "We will be

happy to come," he said at once. "Please take our greetings to your master. We send him all good will."

"Do you think we have made the Governor angry by preaching here?" asked Barnabas when the messenger had gone. "Could it be that he really does want to know about Jesus?"

"We are sent to tell the good news to the Gentiles," Saul reminded him. "Let us pray for wisdom and strength to preach the word boldly to the Governor. May God's power work through us in a special way with this man."

The next day Saul and Barnabas went to the palace. "Take us to your master," they instructed the guards at the gate. "He sent for us."

As they went into the room where the Governor was waiting, Saul noticed an evil-looking man standing in the corner. The Governor motioned the two men to sit down near him.

"Who are you? Where are you from? I want to know what you are preaching to the people about God," said the Governor.

Barnabas introduced himself first and explained that he had been born on the island. When it was Saul's turn to speak, Barnabas was surprised to hear his friend use his Roman name of "Paul." "I suppose it is wise to use a Roman name if you are a Roman citizen as Saul is, since this governor is a Roman official," thought Barnabas. "Perhaps I should also call him Paul."

Paul, as he was called from this time on, wasted no time in preaching to the Governor. "God is a righteous God and

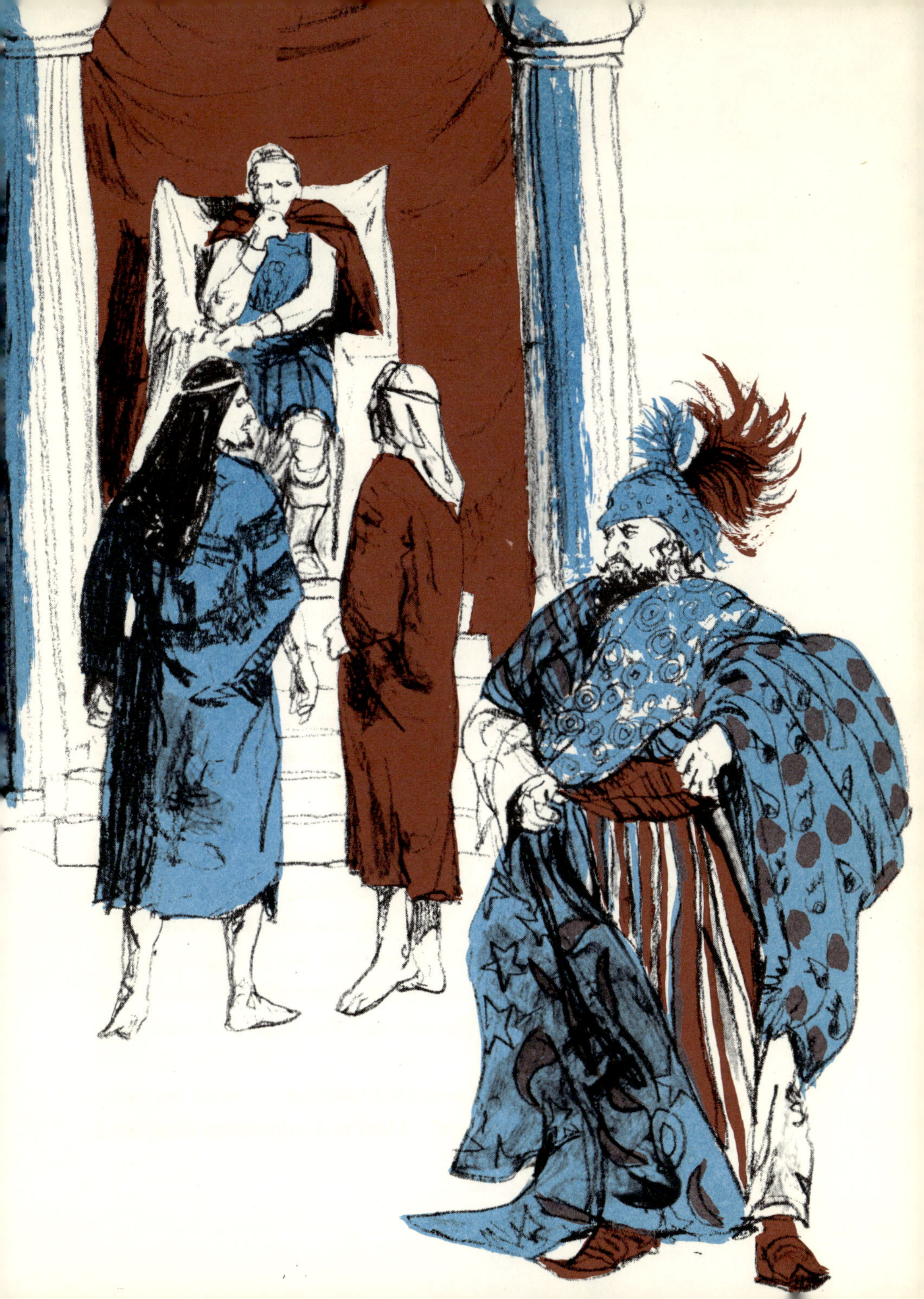

nothing evil can remain in his presence. But all men have done wrong and need his forgiveness. Because God loves all men he sent his Son Jesus Christ, who was killed by sinful men. Then God raised him up, and today Jesus lives and stands at the right hand of God. He died so that all who believe in him might be forgiven."

"Ha! Ha!" growled a voice from behind Paul. He looked around and saw that it was the evil-looking man he had noticed earlier. "This Jesus you are talking about is just a common criminal," said the man. "Everyone knows he was put to death like one. He was crucified! That's what happened to your Jesus person. Pay no attention to this false teacher, O Most High Governor. He is telling nothing but lies."

Paul's eyes blazed. Now that he could get a good look at the man, Paul recognized him to be a magician he had heard about earlier. "He stays close to the Governor and gives him all sorts of advice," Paul had been told.

Suddenly Paul felt strong and sure of what he should say. It was as though someone else was telling him the words to speak. "You fake! You enemy of all that is good! You are full of evil tricks. Why do you try to put stumbling blocks in the way of a man who wants to learn about the living Lord?"

The magician had not expected anything like this! "That's bold talk from a mere traveling preacher," he sneered.

Paul was not finished. "Look now! The hand of the Lord is going to make you blind for a little time."

Everyone in the room watched as the magician began to

shake. He turned to go, but he could not see the way. He groped about, stumbled, and fell to the ground. He begged for someone to take him by the hand and lead him out. Finally, one of the Governor's servants took him away.

The Governor looked at Paul. "Tell me more about this Jesus of Nazareth," he said. "Where is he? How can I know him?"

"He will come to every man who believes on him in faith," answered Paul. Then he told how he himself had tried for many years to win God's favor by obedience to the law. "I tried by my own strength to keep from sinning, and I felt hopeless and defeated. Now I am full of joy, for I know that God forgives me and does not expect me to do the impossible. Thanks be to God who makes my life a never-ending victory in Jesus Christ."

The Governor was silent for a long time. Then he raised his head and looked at Paul as though he were a good friend. "I believe that Jesus is the Christ, the one sent from God," said the Governor. "I accept him as Lord of my life."

"Thanks be to God who gives us the victory through our Lord Jesus Christ," said Barnabas.

"Praise be to God," said Paul.

8
Paul Becomes the Leader

"The time has come for us to leave Cyprus," Paul said one day. "We have stayed here long enough. We should move on to other places where people do not know Jesus Christ."

Soon the three men were ready to leave the island. They bought passage on a ship that would carry them to the mainland. At sailing time Paul saw young Mark standing on the deck looking out across the sea. He did not know that the young boy was wishing he could go back to Jerusalem. Barnabas noticed Mark too, and thought he looked lonely. He went over to where his young cousin was standing. "You look unhappy, boy. What's the matter? Don't tell me you are seasick already!"

"It's not seasickness, Barnabas. It's all this plan about going on to Perga, and then some place else, and on and on. Do we have to travel so far? When are we going back home?"

Barnabas sighed. "You see, Mark, the Lord has told us to go to all the nations of the earth. That means there is no place too far away for us to go if there are people who need to learn the truth about Jesus."

"I don't think there is anything I can do to help you," said Mark. "Oh, Barnabas, I don't want to travel on and on like this. I just want to go back to Jerusalem."

Paul was very disappointed when Barnabas told him of Mark's wish. "This is no time to leave us," said Paul. "He knows I have this awful fever. Surely he could stay with us now, when we need him so badly. But if he is determined to go, let him go."

Mark held to his wish, but he waited until they arrived at the rugged mountain pass which Paul and Barnabas would have to cross to get to a town named Antioch. (This Antioch was a different city from the one where they had worked before starting on their journey.) Then Mark left his two companions and started for home.

Day after day Paul and Barnabas plodded on. Paul's fever grew worse. For a time Barnabas was sure that his friend was going to die in the cold and snow of the mountains. Late one afternoon Barnabas stopped suddenly in the middle of the steep path. He held up his hand for Paul to be quiet.

"I think I hear men's voices coming closer," said Barnabas. "There are robbers in these mountains. Perhaps we should hide somewhere until we see who is coming."

"I'll do whatever you say," said Paul. "I am too cold and tired to try to escape if they are thieves."

The two men huddled together in a tiny cave among the rocks. Sure enough, a group of rough-looking men soon appeared. They passed close by the cave, but never stopped to look inside. "We'll give them plenty of time to get far ahead of us," whispered Barnabas. "That will also give you a chance for a good rest."

Finally the hard trip was over and the travelers arrived at a place where Paul could rest and recover from his illness. When he was able to work again, Paul went with Barnabas to the synagogue in Antioch.

"Will you speak to us?" asked the rulers of the synagogue. As usual, Paul accepted their invitation gladly. "Men of Israel, and all you who worship God, listen to me," he began. He asked his listeners to remember how God had loved them and made them into a nation a long time ago. He reminded them how the nation had turned against God many times and often disobeyed him. Finally he told how God had sent his Son to show all men his great love for them. "God freely offers you forgiveness if you will believe in Jesus Christ," said Paul.

He stopped speaking and looked at the congregation. No one spoke. No one moved. They wanted to hear every word. But did they believe? Would they accept the truth when it was offered to them?

"Beware," Paul warned them. "Believe what I am telling you, or you will be turning away from God's love."

When the service was ended, Paul and Barnabas started to leave the synagogue. "Stay and tell us more about Jesus and his way," said some of the people. "How can we believe unless you teach us more about him?"

The two preachers were surrounded by people who

wanted to ask questions. Some even followed Paul and Barnabas all the way to the house where they were staying. "We must not send them away," said Barnabas. "Let them stay and we will teach them here."

The next Sabbath Paul and Barnabas were asked to speak again in the synagogue. More and more people crowded into the room where the service was to be held. The leaders began to wonder whether or not this was a good thing.

"Look at those Gentiles who are trying to crowd in here," they grumbled. "We must not let these preachers stir up the people with their talk. Listen to them carefully. If what they say does not agree with what our fathers have taught us, then we will speak up and tell them they are wrong."

Paul preached as he had before. He told the crowd that there was hope only in God's love through Jesus Christ.

"I don't believe God would choose such a way to send his Messiah!" shouted a man near the back of the room.

"I agree!" called out another. "Why would God allow his own Son to be put to death like any common criminal?"

"Let Paul speak," insisted a young man near the front. "I want to hear more about Jesus. Is he truly alive?"

"All that is just a story his followers made up," shouted the first man. "You don't expect them to admit that he's dead, do you? They had to invent some story to explain what happened to him."

All over the synagogue people began to yell at Paul. Then they screamed at each other, and at the leaders who tried to quiet them. They shouted louder and louder until Paul suddenly raised his arm and called out in a thundering voice, "We brought the word of God to you first. Since you refuse to accept it, you show that you are not worthy of God's gift. We will leave you and go to the Gentiles. The Lord himself instructed us to do this, and to take his message to the ends of the earth."

Paul and Barnabas pushed their way through the crowded synagogue and stepped outside. They began to preach again in the open air, and the Gentiles crowded around to hear every word. They begged for more when the two men stopped preaching. Many believed in Jesus, and went off to tell their friends about him.

As the days went by, more and more Gentiles heard the word and believed. The rulers of the synagogue began to get frightened. "These two preachers are ruining our congregation," they said. "People who used to worship with us now go out to listen to them. They are even believing this talk about Jesus of Nazareth being the Messiah sent from God."

"You must find some way to silence those men," said some of the women. "We are tired of hearing this nonsense about the rulers of the temple rejecting the Messiah. They knew what they were doing far better than these two traveling preachers. Get rid of them right away!"

Some of the leading men of the town agreed with the women. "Our synagogue was quiet and peaceful before those two came here with their wild stories about Jesus being crucified and raised from the dead. Who knows what will happen if Paul and Barnabas stay. If we don't do something right away, their followers soon will be stronger than we are."

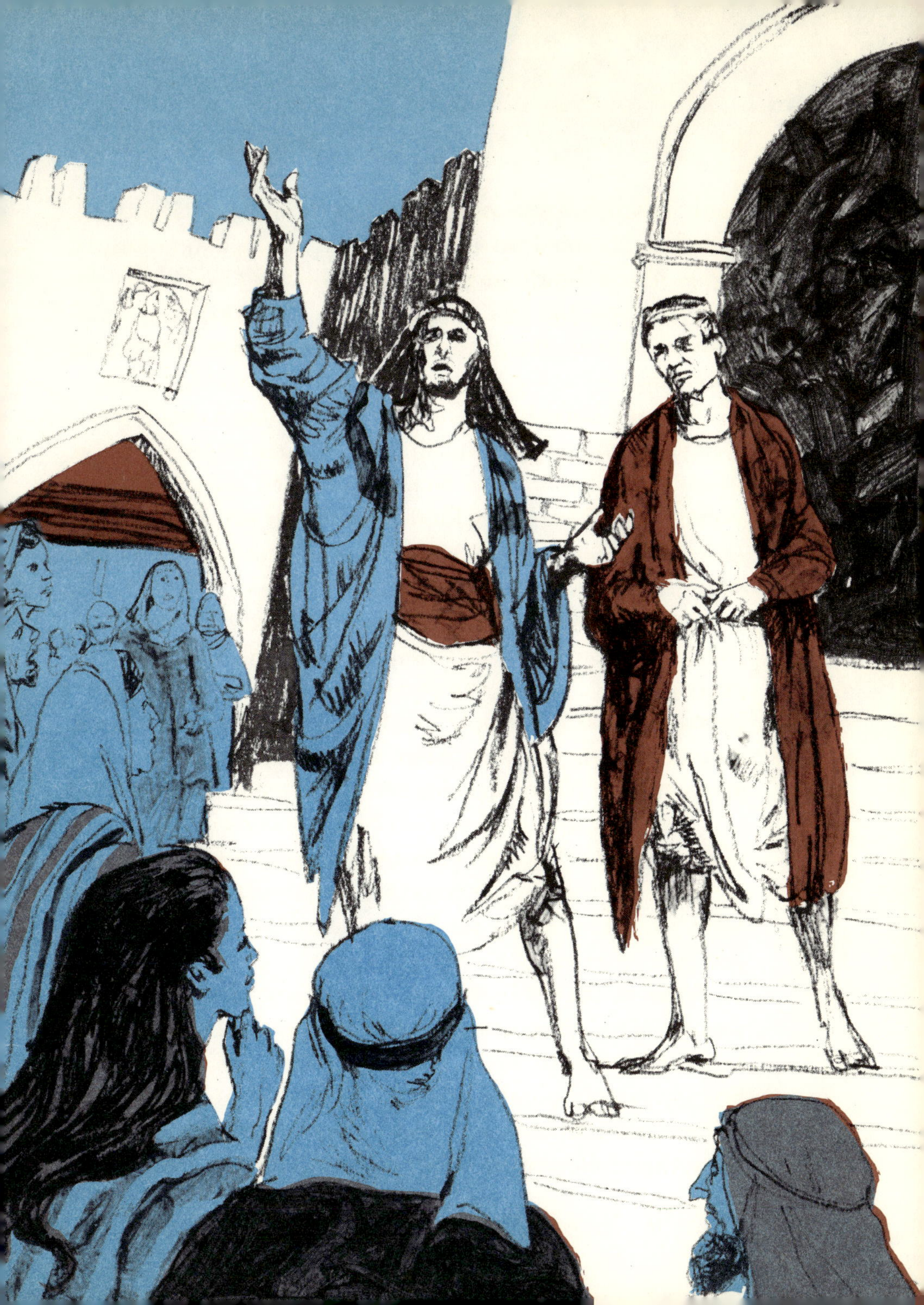

They plotted and planned together how they could get rid of the two men. At first they whispered about it among themselves. Then they made open threats against the preachers. Finally Paul and Barnabas knew they would have to move on.

"It makes me sad to leave them like this," said Barnabas. "Remember what a warm welcome they gave us, and how they invited us to speak in the synagogue when we first arrived?"

"They are just as eager to drive us out and be rid of us now," replied Paul. "Once I would have been very angry with people who treated me like this. But now I am sorry for them. They are turning their backs on God, not on us. We are not losing anything, but they are losing much by refusing to accept God's gift of love."

The two men prepared to leave Antioch. "We'll preach in some other city," said Barnabas. "Our enemies will be rid of us, but they cannot drive out all the people in the city who believe in Jesus. I'm happy that we are leaving behind us many who are filled with God's spirit."

9
Not Gods, but Men!

"Mother! Have they come yet?" Young Timothy ran into the room and set the heavy water jug carefully on the floor. Then he helped himself to a long, cool drink.

Eunice, his mother, brought a basket of fruit to the table. She looked around to see that everything was ready for the guests. "Not yet, Timothy," she replied. "But it's a long journey through the mountain pass and down the valley to Lystra. Paul and Barnabas will be tired and hungry when they do arrive. Run out to the street and watch for them. They may not know which house is ours."

"Why were they chased out of those towns up north?" Timothy wondered as he watched and waited for the two preachers. "Why does this new truth they are teaching make people so angry? I wonder if they will dare to preach here in Lystra. Perhaps they will only rest in our house and then go on."

Paul and Barnabas had been preaching in a town to the

north of Lystra. Once again they had made the synagogue leaders angry and were forced to leave the town when some people threatened to stone them. But they were not coming to Lystra to rest or to take things easy. As they came closer to the city they began thinking about where they would go to preach.

"There is no synagogue in Lystra," said Barnabas. "We'll have to find some other place where people gather."

"The marketplace!" answered Paul at once. "That's where you always find people. We'll go there first thing tomorrow."

"I think we turn this way to go to the house of Eunice, the good Jewish lady who offered to take care of us," said Barnabas. "She has a young son named Timothy."

Just ahead the two men saw a boy peeping at them from the doorway of a house. Suddenly he disappeared. They could hear him calling excitedly, "Mother, come quick! They are here! I'm sure it's Paul and Barnabas coming down the street."

That evening the men sat for a long time in the cool courtyard. They told about their adventures, and about the many people in towns along the way who had become believers in Jesus Christ. Timothy wanted to know all about how they had been stoned and chased out of the synagogues. He asked them to tell again about their long trip through the mountains. He wanted to know exactly what they were going to do in Lystra.

Eunice asked questions about Jesus. She wanted to know

why they were so sure that he was the Messiah. She talked about preaching the good news of God's gift to the Gentiles in Lystra. "The Jews here may make trouble for you," she warned. "There are so few of us here in Lystra that we must guard our religion carefully."

"Tomorrow we will try to find a place where we can begin to preach about Jesus Christ," said Paul. "We are not afraid, for we know we speak only the truth. Do you have friends we can visit? Perhaps they will listen to us first. Later we may find some listeners in the marketplace."

Paul and Barnabas worked hard preaching and teaching to anyone who would listen. Timothy often went with them to help in any way he could. Soon he also began to ask many questions about Jesus, and Paul would always find enough time to answer him.

One day Timothy said, "Tomorrow is a feast day. You can come with me to the marketplace and watch the parade of the gods that are carried from the temple of Jupiter. No one wants to miss seeing that!"

Barnabas smiled and patted Timothy on the shoulder. "We'll go with you to the marketplace, my son. No doubt a great crowd will be gathered there. But we will not be going just to see the gods of Jupiter, I promise you that."

Timothy had trouble going to sleep that night. What did Barnabas mean? Why would anyone go to the market on a feast day if he did not want to see the gods on parade? He finally went to sleep, and dreamed that he was walking right at the front of the parade with Paul and Barnabas. All the people were cheering and shouting wildly at them!

The next morning Timothy was the first one ready to leave the house. "Come on. It's this way," he said, leading Paul and Barnabas along a narrow street behind the market stalls. "Here's the place where you can see best. Get up on the steps there by old Amos the lame beggar. He's always around on feast days. That's when he gets the most money. People feel sorry for him and throw him some coins."

Paul and Barnabas found a place a little higher up on the steps. "Look over there," said Timothy as he tugged at Barnabas' sleeve.

"Shhh," whispered Barnabas. "Listen to Paul. He's going to speak to the crowd."

"Men of Lystra," Paul began, "listen to me. We bring a message to you. We have come to tell you that God has kept his promise to send you a Savior."

"I've heard him preach before," muttered the lame beggar. "That Savior he tells about must be for someone else, not for me."

"God has sent his Son to be the light of the world. Follow him and you will no longer live in darkness. It does not matter whether you are Jew or Gentile, rich or poor, strong or weak." Paul continued, looking straight at the old beggar, who was listening carefully to every word now. "No matter how weak you are, God who is Lord of heaven and earth has power to give you strength."

Paul stood gazing at old Amos. The beggar stared back at him. The crowd grew very quiet. It was almost as though

Paul could hear Amos saying, "Now I believe you. I believe!"

Suddenly Paul commanded in a loud voice, "Stand up straight on your feet!"

Timothy watched as old Amos jumped up, balanced himself for a minute, and then took a step. "Oh, dear! What if he falls," thought Timothy.

But the beggar didn't fall. He took another step, and then another. Soon he was walking about and shouting to the crowd to come and see. More and more people gathered to see the wonderful sight.

Suddenly someone in the crowd looked at Paul standing on the steps, with Barnabas nearby. "They are gods come down to us in the form of men," shouted the man. "Jupiter and Mercury are here with us!"

Almost before they knew what was happening, Paul and Barnabas saw the crowd kneeling down before them. Some boys ran up the steps and threw wreaths of flowers around their necks. For a moment the two men just stood there. They were too surprised to move or speak.

"They think you are gods!" shouted Timothy. "The priest is coming from the temple to bring you a sacrifice. Listen, you can hear the drums and music."

Sure enough, off in the distance Paul could see a procession coming towards them. The priests were leading an ox, and people were bringing more flowers.

Barnabas tore the wreath from his neck and ran into the middle of the crowd. "Stop! Stop!" he yelled. "Why are you doing this? We are only human beings. We are men and not

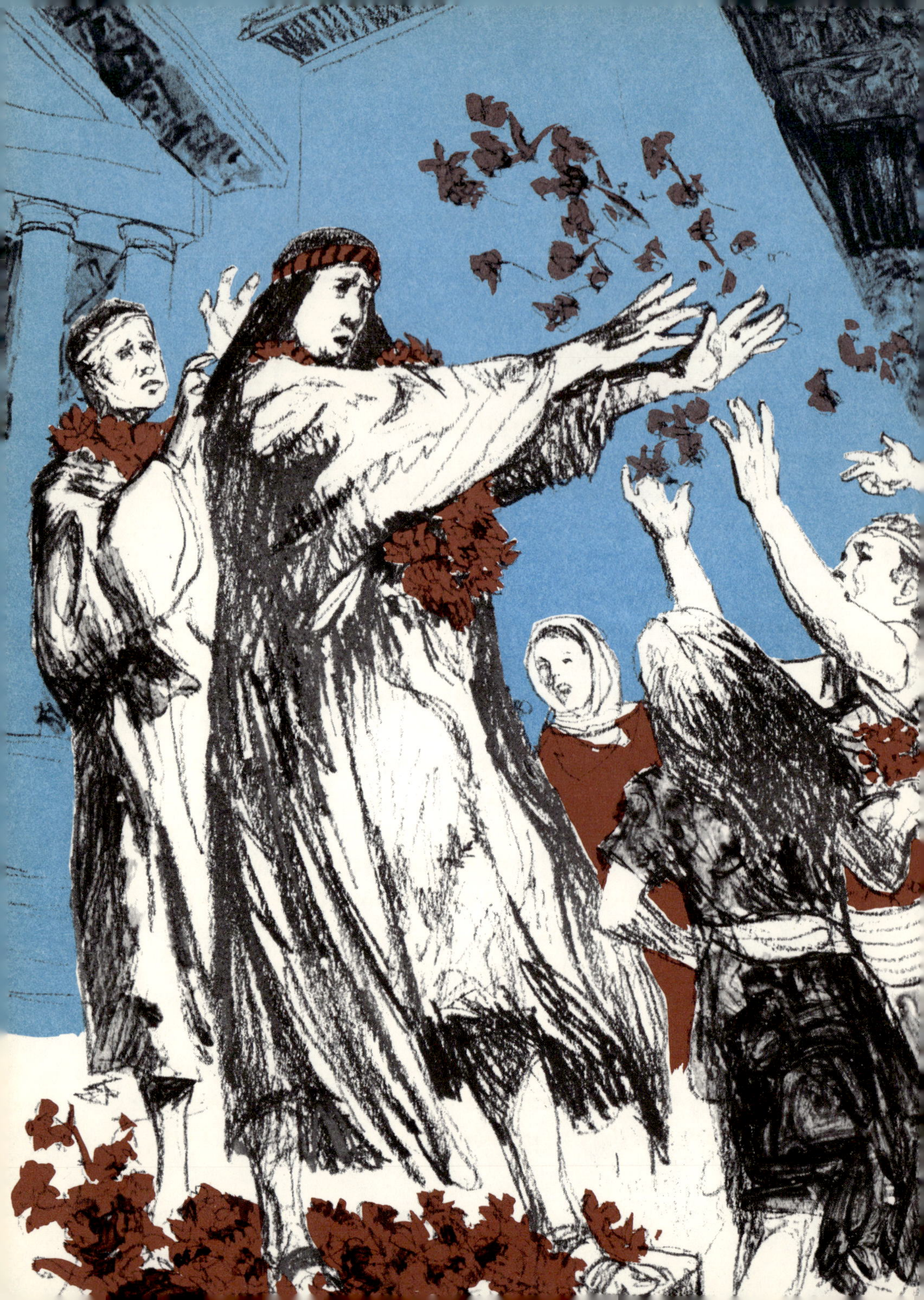

Not Gods, but Men!

gods. There is only one true God, and we serve him. He is the one who has given you all the good things of your life. You must praise and worship only him, not the false gods. Put away your idols. Turn to God in faith."

The crowd began to move off to other parts of the marketplace. "I still think they are gods," some people said. "I wish they would do more wonderful acts. Why do they only talk about a God we cannot see?"

As Timothy pushed his way up the steps to get closer to his friends, he heard several men plotting together. They were huddled in a little group and talked in low voices. Timothy was close enough to hear one of them saying something about Paul. When he heard Paul's name, he stopped to listen.

"Those are the two men, all right," whispered the speaker pointing at Paul and Barnabas. "That one there is Paul. He's the leader. He's the one to get!"

"I'm sure they are the same ones who stirred up all the trouble in our synagogue in Antioch," added another man. "Paul was ill when he came to our town. But as soon as the fever left him, we could not keep him from preaching to everyone who would listen. You're right, he's the one we must get rid of. If we could make the crowd angry enough to turn on them, maybe the people would take care of these two false teachers for us. That way no one could blame us for anything."

Timothy watched as the group joined the crowd, whispering and pointing at Paul and Barnabas. People slowly began to return to where the two preachers were still standing. This time no one shouted praises. No one brought flowers. Instead, people began to curse and scream at Paul and Barnabas. They were angry because they had been foolish enough to treat two human men like gods. "You are liars!" they shouted. "Get out! Go away and leave us to worship our own gods!"

The crowd grew more and more angry as the men who had stirred them up continued to urge them on. Someone picked up a rock and threw it at Paul's head. Another rock, and then another hit Paul. Timothy saw him fall to the ground. He was holding his head and trying to protect himself from the sharp stones.

Timothy was so frightened he didn't know what to do. He looked around for Barnabas, but could not see him anywhere. Timothy did not know that friends had come to the rescue and whisked Barnabas away to a hiding place while the confusion was at its worst.

Paul lay very still on the ground. "See, he doesn't move any longer. He must be dead," someone shouted. "Let's get his body out of here. He won't cause us any more trouble." So they dragged Paul off and left him lying in a heap at the side of a road near the edge of town.

Friends followed the mob and stayed as close as they could to Paul. They waited for everyone else to leave. Then they rushed to him. "Look! He's moving his head. He's trying to speak," exclaimed one friend.

"He's not dead," cried Timothy joyfully. "Paul is alive!"

"Praise be to God," said an older man. "Let's get him away from here at once."

"Bring him to our house," called Timothy. "He will be safe there. I'll run and tell Mother what's happened. She'll know what to do for Paul."

The friends carefully helped Paul to get up on his feet. "Put your arms around our shoulders," said two men. "We'll help you get back into the city where we can care for your injuries."

Later Timothy remembered what he had heard Paul muttering as he lay on the roadside. It had sounded like, "Blessed are you when men persecute you for my sake. Rejoice, and be glad."

"Jesus makes those who believe in him glad even when they're suffering for his sake," Timothy told his mother. "I can't help believing in him when I listen to Paul and see how much he loves his Lord. I think I will be a follower of Jesus someday."

Late that night Paul sat talking with a group of friends. Eunice had cared for his wounds, and Barnabas had come out of hiding to join his companion. "It's too dangerous for you two to stay in Lystra any longer; you must go away in the morning," urged one of the group. "If those men who stirred up the crowd today find out that Paul is alive, they'll come here hunting for you both. They are dangerous enemies because they believe you are a threat to their faith."

"We could go toward the frontier," suggested Barnabas. "Perhaps we would have less trouble there. The people may listen to us and not drive us away. We will come back to Lystra some other time."

Early the next morning, Paul and Barnabas set out along the road leading toward the south. Timothy walked with them as far as the first mile marker. "Will you take me with you someday?" he begged. "I believe that Jesus is the one God promised to send. I believe he is the Lord!"

Paul smiled. "Someday we *will* take you," he promised. "Go back home now, and listen to the teachings of your mother and your grandmother. You can learn much about our faith from them. Then you'll be ready when we come again."

Timothy watched until the two men were out of sight. He turned slowly and started for home. "Someday I will go with them," he thought. "I'll help to tell the good news about Jesus. I want to preach about him, too."

10
A Challenge

News of Paul and Barnabas was carried back to the church in Jerusalem. Mark told what he had seen and heard. Travelers brought reports from Lystra and other towns where the two men had been preaching and teaching. Paul would have been very unhappy to hear what the disciples in Jerusalem were saying.

"We never should have allowed Gentiles to join our fellowship in the first place," said some of the disciples. "Paul and Barnabas should have preached only to the Jews. Then they wouldn't have caused all this trouble."

"They are not the only ones who are in trouble, thanks to their mistake," said one of the older disciples. "We hear that in the synagogues where they preached, the rabbis are having a hard time answering the questions and doubts those two stirred up. If the Gentiles want to believe in God and accept Jesus as their Messiah, then they should follow the Jewish customs as we do. Paul and Barnabas are making it too easy for non-Jews to join our fellowship."

"Who gave them permission to go on this preaching trip in the first place?" others asked. "We should have been the ones to send them out, not that young church in Antioch. They should have talked with us before they went anywhere."

Some of those who had been believers since the earliest days were angry to learn that Paul now was the leader of the trip. "Who does he think he is?" they sneered. "Barnabas at least was one of us. But not Paul! He's quite a newcomer to be taking over as leader."

All this time Paul and Barnabas were preaching and teaching. They went back to visit believers in some of the towns where they had preached earlier on their trip. Then one day they decided it was time to sail for their home church in Antioch.

When the two men arrived, their friends listened anxiously as they told about the crowds who had come to listen. "The power of God's Spirit worked through us to bring both Jews and Gentiles to the true faith," reported Paul. "We left many faithful believers to carry on the work we started."

"How did the Gentiles act when you told them that God loves them as well as the Jews?" someone asked.

Joyfully Barnabas told how the Gentiles often were more eager to listen than were their Jewish brothers. A few of Paul's friends wanted to ask questions about this.

"You say that the Gentiles are not required to follow our customs and obey the laws of Moses. Doesn't that make it too easy for them to believe in Jesus as their Lord?" they asked.

A Challenge

"Somehow it does not seem right that we should obey when they don't have to."

"It's right for Jews to obey the commands of God that have come to us in the laws of Moses," Paul explained once again. "The Gentiles may do so if they wish. But faith in Jesus Christ, and being willing to live in his way of love, are the most important things for all believers."

One day visitors from Jerusalem arrived in Antioch. "Welcome, brothers," the people greeted them. "It's good to see you. What news do you bring from our friends in Jerusalem? Is the church there growing stronger? Have you come to bring us advice? Come and speak to our congregation in the synagogue. Everyone will want to hear what you have to say."

After the people had gathered, one of the visitors stood up to speak. "Peace be to you, our brothers. We in Jerusalem have heard of your good work here in Antioch. We have also heard that many Gentiles have by faith become believers and joined your fellowship." The speaker paused and looked around. "I can see that this is so, and it is good."

"It is good that we can all be brothers in the Lord," someone whispered. "We are happy to be one fellowship in Christ, with no need to set the Gentiles apart from us Jews."

The speaker did not look very happy. When he started to talk again, Paul glanced at Barnabas and frowned. Both men wondered what was to come next.

"The reason I have come here," the speaker went on, "is to remind you that no man can set aside the commands of

God. It is not right for you to allow some people to join our fellowship without making them obey the requirements set down for the rest of us. This is a very serious matter because many Gentiles are asking to become believers. Therefore, your brothers in Jerusalem have sent you this warning. Unless the Gentiles agree to obey the laws of Moses and accept our customs, they must be told that God's love and forgiveness shown in Jesus Christ is not for them."

At first no one in the congregation said a word. If what this man said was true, then God's love was not free to all men. It was for obedient Jews only—not for Gentiles.

Paul and Barnabas jumped to their feet. They were ready to defend what they had preached to the Gentiles about God's gift of love being free for all people. They argued with their visitors from Jerusalem for a long time, but no one would give in.

"It is foolish to argue this way," said Barnabas. "These men who have come here are saying only what they were told to tell us."

"Then we must go to Jerusalem," Paul responded. "I will tell the leaders there how wonderful it is to live freely the life of love that Jesus teaches. I will not stand by and let them deny such a precious gift to any man simply because he will not first agree to become a Jew."

Paul was anxious to settle this question once and for all. On the trip to Jerusalem, he told Barnabas about his early days as a young student. "I tried harder than anyone to find favor with God by keeping the whole Law. I wanted to do everything I could to live in a way pleasing to him. But it was no use. For the more I failed to keep the Law, the more I knew I needed help. Now I have God's forgiveness as a free gift. I am happy because I am saved by faith in Jesus Christ. No one who believes in him can have this gift taken away. I'll tell that to the leaders in Jerusalem. They *must* believe me, Barnabas."

After several days, Paul and Barnabas reached the city. Never had they faced a harder job than the one they had before them. Both men prayed for God's Spirit to give them wisdom and patience. Back home in Antioch their brothers were also praying for them.

The two preachers went into the upper room where the church leaders were waiting for them. "Welcome, brothers. Peace be to you!" Peter and James welcomed the tired travelers from Antioch. Others welcomed them, too, but not quite so warmly. Paul and Barnabas had not come to Jerusalem to pay a friendly visit. They had come to settle a dispute.

At first everyone wanted to hear news from Antioch. They asked questions about friends and relatives whom Paul and Barnabas had met on their preaching trip. Paul got very excited as he talked. "The Gentiles crowded in to hear us preach that Jesus is Lord," he said. "Many of them believed and joined the fellowship."

While Paul was still talking, some of the disciples began to whisper in the back of the room. Several looked very angry. Finally one of the older men rose to speak. "All this sounds very good," he began. "But you must tell those Gentile converts that they can be part of our fellowship only on one condition. They must first accept our Jewish customs and obey the laws of Moses."

The argument was on. Barnabas reminded the group that wherever he and Paul had gone, they had preached first to the Jews. "But in one town after another, they turned us away! It was the Gentiles who listened to us. They begged us to stay and tell them more about the truth we had come to preach. What were we to do? Would you want us to turn our backs on the people who were searching for the very message about God we were sent to preach?"

"Just what *did* you tell these people?" asked Peter.

A Challenge

Paul got up to speak. He waited until everyone in the room was quiet. He remembered that day on the Damascus road when Jesus said to him, "You will be my witness . . ." Paul prayed silently that he would be able to be a true witness to these friends and brothers.

"Barnabas and I preached faith in Jesus Christ," Paul stated simply. Then he told about the wonderful works God had done through them while they were on their long journey.

Paul talked on and on. "You know yourselves that God chose Peter to be the first to take the message of God to the Gentiles. Barnabas and I preached the same message. We have seen God's Spirit at work among the Gentiles. I agree with Peter. Why should we ask them to carry a burden that we are not able to carry ourselves? That burden of trying to obey the law was like a prison to us before Christ's coming. Now I am out of that prison! I do not mean that I am set free to do whatever I please, mind you. Instead, I am free to live as a true son of God through faith in Jesus. I preach that all who have this faith are true sons of God, no matter whether they are Jews or Gentiles, rich or poor, free men or slaves, men or women!"

Then everyone began to talk at once. Finally James stood up. "Brothers," he said, "will you listen to me? No one wants to make it harder for Gentiles to believe in Jesus. We do not want to turn them away from God. I propose that we send letters to churches where Gentiles have joined with Jews as believers in Christ. Let us remind them of a few main points of the law which ought to be kept. We will say that we do not expect them to follow every single one of our Jewish customs in order to be a part of the church."

"A letter is a good idea," the group agreed. "But let's be careful to say exactly what we mean. We must make a decision that every Christian can agree to, and then we won't have to change it again."

Paul and Barnabas were happy to take a copy of the letter back to their church in Antioch. They could hardly wait to get home to tell the good news to the Gentiles there. As soon as they arrived, people came to find out what had happened in Jerusalem. "Must we become Jews? Will we have to leave the fellowship if we do not obey all the laws of Moses?"

"We have a letter from the church leaders in Jerusalem," replied Barnabas. "It will answer your questions. Listen while I read it to you."

Paul was pleased to see his people happy once more. "We are free now to live as Christ's own people," they said. "Teach us more about the Lord Jesus, Paul. We want to follow his way of love faithfully."

11
Come Over and Help Us!

For a time Paul and Barnabas were busy and happy working in the Antioch church. They were glad to do the work the Lord had sent them there to do. One day Paul was talking with Barnabas. "I've been thinking a lot about the followers we left behind in the cities where we preached on our last trip. Why don't we go back to visit them? I want to know how they're getting along."

"Shall we take Mark with us again?" asked Barnabas.

"Not Mark!" exclaimed Paul. "He would go only halfway the last time. I'll never take him on a trip with me again."

"But Mark is a good helper," Barnabas insisted. "I'm going to take him along if we go on this trip."

Paul was upset. "If that's the way you want it, you can take Mark and go your own way. I'll take our friend Silas with me."

"Very well," replied Barnabas, disappointed. "Mark and I will go back to Cyprus. You and Silas can go wherever you please."

One place Paul especially wanted to visit was Lystra. On the way there he told Silas about his young friend Timothy. "He will be a good helper to take along with us. I love that boy almost like a son."

The Christians in Lystra were excited when they heard that Paul was coming back to visit them. Timothy, now a young man, was waiting and watching for his good friend. He welcomed the travelers, gave them water to wash their feet, and brought fruit for them to eat. He took care of them just as the head of a house should do. At the same time, he was asking one question after another. Where were they going? Why hadn't Barnabas come? What had happened in Jerusalem?

The next day Paul said to Timothy's mother, "We would like to take Timothy along to help us in our work. Would you be willing to let him come?"

Eunice smiled. "I know Timothy is eager to go with you. He would have been very unhappy if you had not asked him. I'll miss him very much, but I'm willing to let my son go with you."

Not long afterwards it was time for the three men to leave Lystra. Eunice walked with them to the town gate. She said good-bye once more, and watched until Timothy was out of sight down the dusty road.

"I hope you'll always remember how much you owe to your mother, Timothy," said Paul. "She is a sincere believer, like your grandmother Lois. They have taught you much on which you can build your own faith."

The men traveled many miles. They often were tired and

hot on the dry roadways. Sometimes they shivered from the freezing cold in the mountain passes. One day Paul became very ill with a high fever. To make matters worse, he was not sure that he knew just what God wanted him to do. He kept asking himself over and over again, "Should we have come this way? Why have I not been able to find a place where I can speak out for God? What does he want us to do? Where does God want us to go?"

Paul grew weaker and weaker. Timothy cared for him day and night, but Paul did not get better. "I've done all I can," said Timothy at last. "We must get help for Paul or he may die."

In the town where they were stopping Timothy found a doctor named Luke. He agreed to come and see what could be done to cure Paul's fever. Luke brought herbs from which he made some medicine for Paul to drink. When his patient began to feel better, Luke asked him, "Are you one of the Jewish preachers?"

Here was Paul's chance to tell him about Jesus. Quickly he began to tell Luke about the good news. Luke listened carefully. Even after it was time for him to go, he stayed on asking questions. "I would like to know more about this Jesus," he said when he finally got up to leave. "I will come to see you again tomorrow. Now you must rest."

The next day Paul could hardly wait for Luke to come. "God has come to us in the man Jesus of Nazareth," he began. "Our prophets told of his coming. Our rabbis waited for him. When he came, men killed him for they did not believe that he was the Son of God. But God raised him up, and now Jesus is alive! He offers us forgiveness and a new life if we will believe in him. This is why I must get well quickly. I have to get on with my work."

"You can't get up until I tell you," said Luke. "I want to be sure that your fever will not return. But I'll come to see you every day. Now tell me more about Jesus."

One day Luke said, "I have news for you, Paul. Wait a minute! You think I am going to tell you that you are well enough to get up and go to work! That's only part of my news." Paul had started to get up from his bed, but Luke stopped him. "I also want to tell you that I believe in Jesus

Christ. I accept God's love and forgiveness. I want to join you in the fellowship of believers."

Paul was delighted. His illness had not kept him from preaching to his doctor. God could use even a sick man to witness to his power and love!

"I wish the people of my homeland could hear this news about Jesus," said Luke. "I'm sure they would listen to the truth and believe, just as I have."

Paul was not yet sure where God wanted him to go. "I'll have to wait. Surely God will tell me when the time is right."

One night Paul had a dream. In it he saw a man standing before him and calling out, "Come over to Macedonia and help us."

Paul decided that this was God's way of telling him to go to Macedonia, Luke's homeland. "We must hurry and find a ship to take us there," he urged the others.

Luke agreed to go with Paul and the others as far as the city of Philippi. "I can find a place there where you can live, and then you can meet many of my friends," Luke told them.

When the men arrived in Philippi, Timothy thought he could have spent the first day just looking at the sights. There was a Roman forum, Greek temples, beautiful statues of the gods, and fine shops on interesting streets. "It's so different from Lystra," he said.

On their first Sabbath day in Philippi, Paul started out with the others to find the place where the Jews of the city worshiped. There was no synagogue, but Paul knew that the Jews would be sure to gather in some place for prayer. Soon they discovered a small group of women gathered on the riverbank.

Paul introduced himself and his friends, and asked permission to speak. At first the women listened politely without saying anything. Then one of them, named Lydia, began to ask questions. "I am a Gentile, as you may know," she said. "For a long time I've worshiped the one true God along with my Jewish friends. Was Jesus sent from God to bring forgiveness to people like me, too?"

The men told them that Jesus came to show God's love for all men, including Gentiles. They went on to tell how he had been put to death in Jerusalem. "But God raised him up and Jesus is alive," said Paul. "We know this is true, for many people have seen him, and he has talked with them."

Paul was pleased to find that many of the women believed the good news. Lydia was one of those who asked to join the fellowship. "Please come and stay in my home," she begged. "It's very large. There's plenty of room for all of you. Then you can tell me more about Jesus and his way of love."

Paul and the others preached every day wherever they could gather people who would listen. Many citizens of Philippi became Christians. One day on their way to the marketplace the men saw a group gathered around a poor slave girl. "Pay me a coin and I'll tell your fortune," she was calling to the crowd.

A man stayed nearby the girl. "Step up and buy a fortune," he shouted. "Only one little coin to buy your fortune."

Paul stopped and glared angrily at the girl's owner. But

the man only went on yelling louder, "Come buy your fortune!"

Suddenly the girl turned around and saw Paul. She ran to him and began pulling at his arm. Then she pointed at Paul and the other men as she shrieked in a wild voice, "These men are servants of the most high God. They have come to tell us how we can be saved!"

Paul felt sorry for the girl for he realized she had an evil spirit which made her guess the future. Gently he took her hand from his arm and walked quickly away. He did not want to start any trouble here.

Almost every day Paul and his friends had to pass the place where the slave girl stood selling fortunes. Each time she ran after them and cried out, "These men are God's servants! Listen to them!"

Paul became disturbed when the same thing happened day after day. "People may think we are paying her to call attention to us. We must put a stop to this." So the next time the girl ran after them, Paul turned around and looked straight at her. "In the name of Jesus Christ, I order the evil spirit to come out of you!"

The slave girl moaned and stopped shouting. She looked around at her owner in fear. "Buy a fortune," he kept on yelling to the crowd. But the girl did not say anything. She could not tell any more fortunes. Her strange powers were gone.

Paul watched as the crowd began to move away. No one would waste a coin on a fortune-teller who could not tell for-

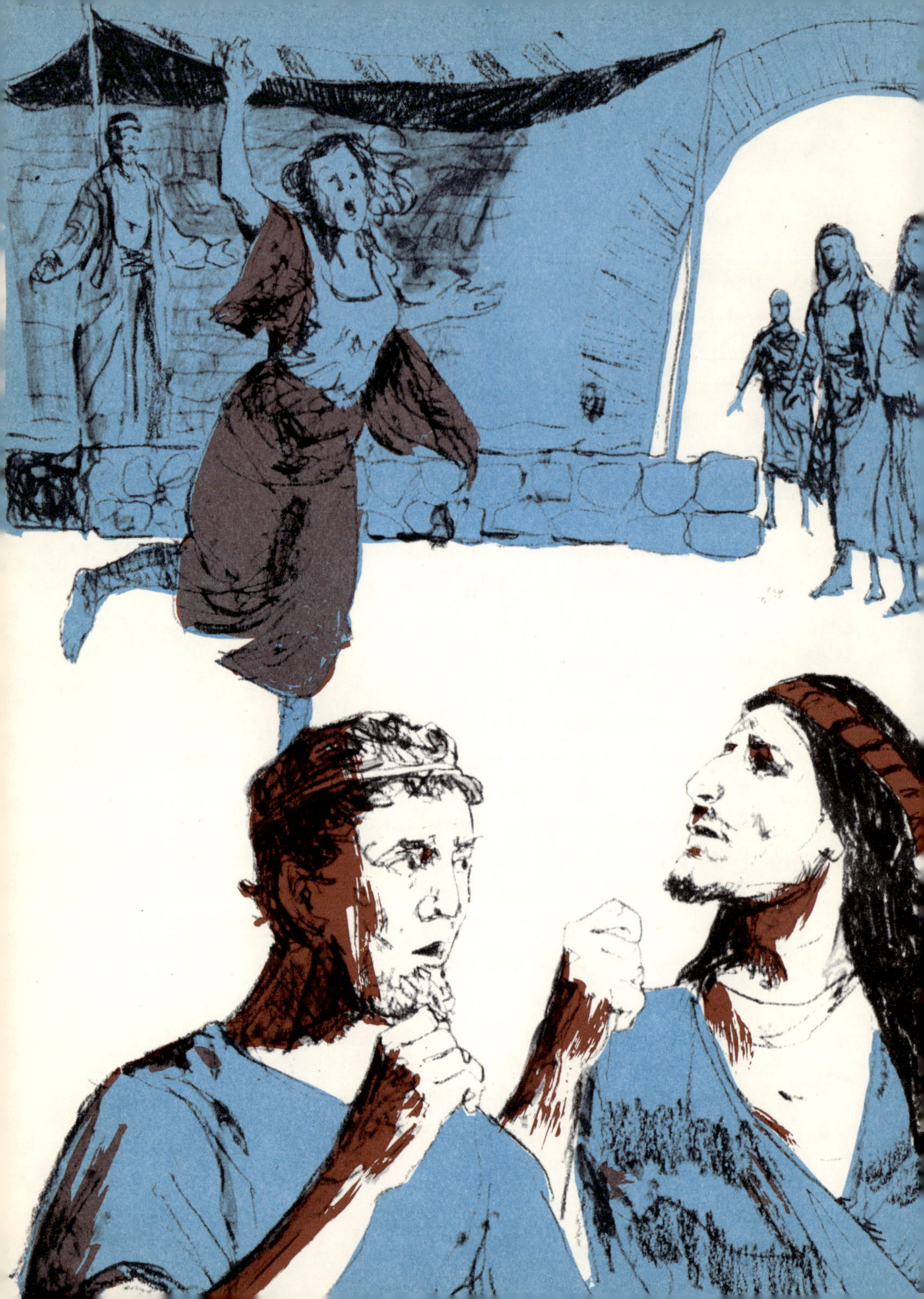

tunes. The girl's owner was furious. His money-making scheme was ruined.

"Come along, Silas. Let's get out of here," said Paul. The two men started hurrying across the marketplace, but the owner and his friends ran after them. They grabbed Paul and Silas and dragged them before the Roman leader of the city.

"These men are Jews, and they are causing trouble in our city," the owner told the officials. "They are teaching customs that are against our laws. We are Romans, and we cannot follow such customs." Then the crowd and the officials tore the clothes off Paul and Silas. The two men were given a severe beating and thrown into jail. The jailer put them into an inside cell and fastened their feet between heavy blocks of wood.

Late that night Paul and Silas sat alone in their cell. Neither one knew what might happen when they were taken to face the city rulers again the next day. But somehow, they weren't afraid. They did not want another beating, but they both knew they could take any punishment for the sake of Jesus.

Silas began to sing, and Paul joined in. The other prisoners listened in great surprise. "Who ever heard of anyone singing in prison? Weeping and cursing is what we always hear, not singing!"

But Paul and Silas continued:
> Blessed is he who comes in the name of the Lord.
> O give thanks to the Lord for he is good;
> For his steadfast love endures for ever!

The two men sang all the hymns of praise to God they could remember. "If I live through this," thought Paul, "it is so that I can go on preaching Christ. If I die, I will not lose anything for I shall be with my Lord. Thanks be to God who gives us the victory through our Lord Jesus Christ. Praise God that he allows us to suffer for Jesus' sake."

The night grew hotter and hotter. Everything was very still. "There's a strange feeling in the air," said one of the prisoners. "It was like this the last time an earthquake hit Philippi."

Suddenly there was a frightening, rumbling sound. It grew louder and louder, and then the whole prison began to shake. Windows broke loose, doors were knocked from their fastenings, and the prisoners' chains fell off. After the noise had stopped, Paul and Silas looked around. The door of their own cell was standing wide open!

"Bring lights!" Paul heard the jailer shout. "Don't let the prisoners escape. I'll have to kill myself if they do!" When the jailer saw the prison door standing wide open, he panicked and drew his sword to kill himself.

"Stop, we are all here. Don't harm yourself," Paul cried. The jailer ran to Paul. He was shaking so much from fright that he fell on the ground. Finally he was able to speak and asked, "How can I be saved?"

Paul answered him in a steady, clear voice, "Believe in the Lord Jesus Christ and you will be saved."

The jailer then did a strange thing. He invited Paul and Silas to come with him to his house. "Here is food for you to eat. I will wash your wounds and give you clean clothes. Now tell me more about Jesus. I want to believe in him."

Paul and Silas told all about Jesus and how he came to bring God's love and forgiveness to all men who would believe in him. "Is it too late for me and my family to be baptized?" asked the jailer. "God has given us faith to believe all that you have told us. Jesus is Lord!"

That morning the messenger from the city rulers came to the jailer's house. There he found Paul and Silas sitting at the table dressed in the jailer's own clothes. They were joyfully celebrating the new-found faith of the whole family who had been baptized into the fellowship.

The two men watched anxiously as the jailer read the message. He looked at the prisoners. "The rulers of the city say that I am to set you free," he told them. "You may leave whenever you please. Blessings on your journey."

"Wait a moment," said Paul. "Yesterday we were publicly beaten before we had been found guilty of any crime. Then we were thrown into prison. Furthermore, we are Roman citizens and we have not been allowed to speak in our own defense. Now they want to get rid of us as quietly as possible. No indeed! Let those who put us here come and let us out. We refuse to sneak away like common criminals."

When the city rulers learned all this, they hurried to the prison. "We are sorry for what we did to you," they apologized. "We did not know that you are citizens of Rome. We beg your forgiveness. Please come with us and we will lead you out of this prison."

Once again Paul and Silas were free men. "It won't be wise for us to stay in this city much longer," said Paul. "Let's go to Lydia's house and say good-bye to our friends."

"You should leave at once, Paul," Luke insisted when the two men arrived at the house. "I'll stay here in Philippi. It is safe for me, for this is my home. Peace be to you and God keep you safe on your journey."

Paul, Silas, and Timothy started off again to find another place where they could preach for God. Where were they to go this time? "We will go wherever God's people are still waiting to hear the good news," said Paul. "No place is too far away for us to go. We will witness for our Lord to the ends of the earth."

12
With Friends in Corinth

Paul and his friends traveled for many weeks and preached in many places. Sometimes the people were glad to hear about Jesus Christ. In other places the officials blamed Paul for causing trouble in their city. "They are breaking the laws of the Roman Emperor by saying there is another king, by the name of Jesus," one officer said. That caused such an uproar that Paul's friends sent him away to another place for his own safety.

Finally Paul reached the city of Corinth. Both Silas and Timothy had stayed behind in another town until Paul could send for them to join him. In Corinth Paul met Aquila and his wife Priscilla who were the owners of a tentmaking shop. They offered him a chance to earn his living by making tents with them, and Paul went to work at once.

One day Paul pushed aside the piece of heavy canvas on which he had been working. He leaned back against the wall and stretched his tired arms. "There, Aquila. That piece is finished. What shall I start on next? Will we be able to finish another tent before sundown?"

Aquila looked up from his work in another corner of the shop. "Take a rest, Paul," he suggested. "You can't work too long on a hot day like this. You'll be too tired to preach tomorrow in the synagogue."

Paul got up and walked to the door of the shop. "My dear friend," he said, "I can't ever repay you and your good wife for all you have done for me. You've given me work to do and a place to live. You've shared your food and everything you have with me. Because of you I am free to preach here in Corinth."

"Don't worry about repaying us, Paul. You are our dearest friend. And besides, you've often worked more than your share. What's more, you have taught us to know Jesus Christ as we never did before."

Paul smiled at Aquila. "You're a real friend. I thank God for you and Priscilla in all my prayers."

Just then Priscilla entered the shop. "A shipload of goat hair has arrived in the harbor," she said to her husband. "The messenger says you should go at once if you want to buy some of it."

Aquila put aside his work. "Will you come with me, Paul?" he asked. "You can help me decide whether or not this shipment will make better tents than that last one. I am sure the merchant cheated me by charging twice what the stuff was worth."

Paul nodded his head. "I'll be glad to go with you. Old

Hilkiah who taught me to make tents was a good judge of leather and goat hair. He showed me how to test for good strong material. No one ever cheated him!"

The two men hurried along the crowded streets leading to the docks. Suddenly they saw a parade of strange-looking people coming towards them. Paul watched some men jumping around like clowns. He saw other men and women wearing long, white robes. One of them carried a lamp shaped like a golden boat. Another held a palm tree made of gold above his head. One person was dressed to look like a cow. Another looked like a monster with a long neck. At the end of the parade Paul saw priests carrying the statue of a god. He watched the people crowding closer to the priests, trying to touch their robes and get a magic blessing.

"What a pity that so many follow after these false gods," said Aquila. "Look how they push to get closer."

Paul continued watching for a few minutes. "Only God himself can make such men know how foolish they are," he said. "This city is full of people like that, and some are even worse. God has sent me to preach Jesus Christ to them so that someday they will know that there is only one true God. Come along, Aquila. I can't stand here and watch them. Let's go on down to the ship. The harbor always reminds me of home. I loved to play around the docks when I was a boy in Tarsus."

A few days later as Paul sat working on some canvas, he heard a familiar voice calling. "Peace be to you, brother Paul. Where are you?"

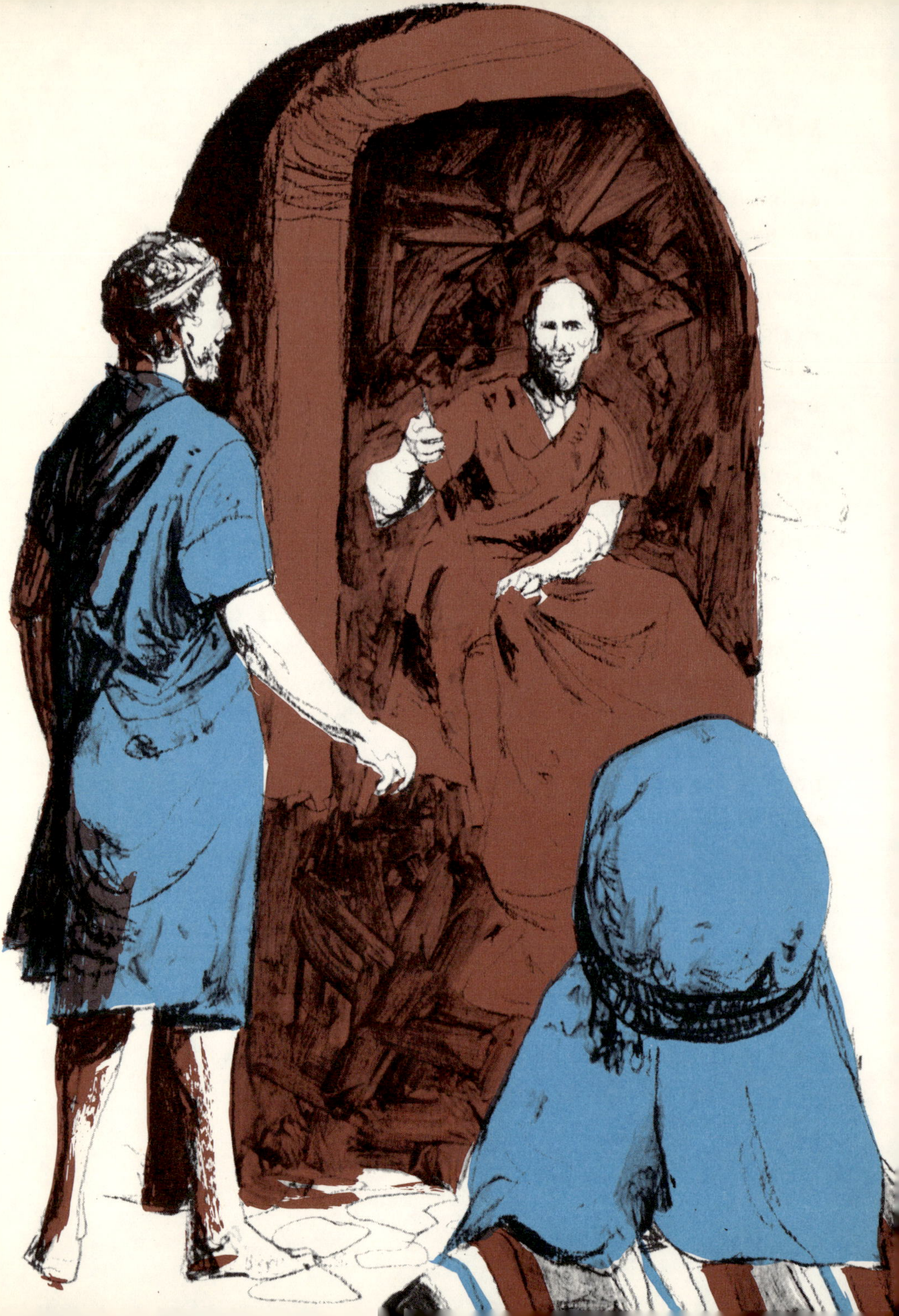

"Timothy!" exclaimed Paul. "And Silas! How good to hear your voices. Here I am, in the shop. Come and tell me about my friends in Macedonia. Are they faithful to Jesus' way? Are the churches growing in number? Is there a warm welcome for Gentiles who want to join the fellowship?"

Silas threw up his hands. "Wait a minute! One question at a time, Paul. We just arrived and we're tired from our long trip."

Paul could scarcely wait while Priscilla brought water for the travelers to wash off the dust of the road. Then food was placed on the table and the men began to eat.

"Tell Paul about the gift first," begged Timothy. "I want to see his face when he hears about it, Silas."

"Gift? What gift?" asked Paul. "I want to hear about my brothers in Christ. Did anyone send me any messages?"

"This will answer both questions," said Silas. He pulled a bag of money from his robe and handed it to Paul. "It's a gift from your friends. They want to help spread the good news of Jesus. It's their way of thanking you for all you've done to make Jesus known to them."

"Praise God for his wonderful works," said Paul. "Now I'll be able to spend all my time preaching and teaching without being a burden to anyone here in Corinth."

"I'm glad for you, Paul," said Aquila. "But I'm going to lose a good tentmaker."

As the weeks went by, Paul preached more boldly than ever before. People crowded into the synagogue to hear him. "Jesus of Nazareth is truly the Messiah God promised to send to us," he proclaimed. "It is true that he was not born as a rich king. It is true that he was put to death by wicked men. But God in his power raised up Jesus to life again."

Sometimes Paul had to stop preaching while those who were listening shouted out questions. "Do you expect us to believe such foolishness? Would all this have happened to God's own Son?"

Paul was quick with his answers. "Remember that you are only sinful men. What seems like God's foolishness to you is wiser than all your human wisdom. It is only through faith in Jesus Christ that you can believe and accept God's gift of love. Only God can make you able to live in a way that pleases him."

Many who listened to Paul believed him and became followers of Jesus. This made some of the Jews very angry. "Leave our synagogue if you are going to preach these things!" they demanded.

"Very well," said Paul. "I will leave. But I know that I preach the truth. You must take the blame for refusing to believe it. I shall go and preach to the Gentiles. They are glad to listen."

One of the Gentiles, a follower of Jesus, offered his house to Paul for a meeting place. "It's right next door to the synagogue," he said. "The Jews will not be able to forget you when they see us gathering there to listen to you preach."

The men of the synagogue watched Paul's congregation growing stronger and larger. "It's time that we stopped this man," they decided. "He has even persuaded some of the leaders of our synagogue to believe that Jesus is the Messiah."

Some of Paul's friends warned him that these Jews were plotting against him. "Perhaps I should leave Corinth," thought Paul. "I don't want to cause any more trouble."

Paul prayed that the Lord would help him know what he should do. One night the answer seemed to come to him clearly. The Lord said, "Do not be afraid. Keep on speaking and do not give up, for I am with you and no one shall harm you. There are many people in this city who are faithful to me."

Now Paul was sure that God wanted him to stay in Corinth. He began to think of nothing but preaching. For many months he taught God's word to all who would listen. Men who had been worshiping false gods turned to the one true God. Christ's power gave many the faith to believe in him as the one sent from God.

Meanwhile Paul knew that the Jews were trying to find some way to silence him. Finally they had a plan. One day they boldly walked into the house where Paul was preaching and dragged him off to court. "This man is persuading people to worship God in a way that breaks the law. He must be punished," they charged.

Before Paul had a chance to defend himself, the ruler of the city said, "If this man has committed a crime, tell me what it is. Has he broken a Roman law? Speak up! I'm a busy man."

Paul listened to hear how the Jews would answer. But they didn't know what to say. They could not name any law that Paul had broken.

Paul smiled as the ruler waved them away impatiently. "When you can name his crime or tell me what law he's broken, I will hear your case. But I have no time for your silly quarreling over your own religious laws. Get out! Leave the court, for I have nothing more to say to you."

Later that night Paul sat talking with his friends. "This is a great victory for you," said Aquila. "Now you can stay here in Corinth as long as you like. Your enemies won't dare risk any more plots against you."

"The victory is from God," said Paul. "It is Christ and not I who won today. It is no longer I who live and work; it is Christ who lives in me."

Paul went on with his work in Corinth. He began to receive news about some of the churches he had visited with Barnabas in earlier years. He learned that many followers of Jesus were being faithful even when it was hard for them. Such news made Paul glad. But when he heard that in Galatia some followers had turned away from the true gospel, Paul was distressed.

"I wish you could go and visit that church yourself," said Silas one day. "They need your advice."

Paul jumped to his feet. "Yes, they do need my advice. And I'm going to give it to them! Silas, bring the reed pen and some ink. Get ready to write a letter to the church in Galatia."

Silas sharpened the pen point. Paul walked up and down, trying to decide what to say. "I, Paul, was sent to preach to you by Jesus Christ and God the Father—not by anyone else. I am surprised to hear that you have turned away from the true gospel of Jesus Christ. In this letter I am telling you again what I preached when I was with you. The only way to find favor with God is through faith in Jesus Christ, and not just by doing what the law requires of you.

"The law only shows you what wrongdoing is. Jesus shows us how much we need God's gift of forgiving love. Faith in Christ makes you free men. But this is no excuse to do wrong. Let love make you serve one another. The whole law adds up to this one commandment: 'Love your neighbor as yourself.'"

Silas wrote all that Paul dictated. "Now I want to add a personal note. Give me the pen, Silas. The only thing that counts is that they believe in Christ and gladly live in love and obedience to God."

One day Paul called Aquila and Priscilla to tell them

about a plan he had. "For a long time I've wanted to go to preach in Ephesus. But first I want to visit my friends in Jerusalem. Will you come with me as far as Ephesus, and stay there until I return? Then we can work together to preach the gospel in that great city."

Paul knew that it would not be easy for his two friends to leave their home, their business, and all their friends. "Nothing is more important than helping to spread the gospel," Aquila reminded his wife. "I guess we can make tents in Ephesus as well as here in Corinth. We'll find new friends there. Christ is our life. Let's go with Paul to serve the Lord."

Finally one day everyone was ready. Paul, with Aquila and Priscilla, sailed for Ephesus. His two friends stayed in that city while Paul went on to Jerusalem. "I'll return to you if God wills," said Paul as he left them and started off. "Peace be to you both from God our Father."

13
At Work in Ephesus

Paul visited his friends in Jerusalem. Many weeks later he stood on the deck of a ship returning to the city of Ephesus. "If this wind holds, we will make port in one more day," said the captain. "We are about here, and we will land here." Paul looked at the map where the captain's finger pointed to Ephesus.

"What a city!" continued the captain. "People come there by sea and by land from all over the world. Most of them want to see the temple of the goddess Diana. I always make a sacrifice to her myself when I land safely. It pays to keep the gods happy if you want to avoid getting shipwrecked. I guess you will be going to worship at her statue, too. You'll be just in time for the big festival in her honor."

Paul looked angry. "I worship only the one true God," he replied. "Gods made by men's hands are no gods at all. They have no power to save anyone. Only the one God can do that."

The captain shrugged his shoulders. "That's what you

say! If you know what's good for you, don't risk making the gods angry by such talk."

Paul was happy to see Aquila and Priscilla waiting for him when the ship docked in Ephesus. "We've been busy teaching God's way while you were gone," they told him. "We did our best, but the people want you to come and preach about Jesus."

Paul found a big crowd waiting on the first day when he went to the synagogue. At last he was going to preach to Jews who would listen to his message about Jesus! These people really wanted to hear what he had to say.

After a few months, however, Paul found that some of the Jews were beginning to make trouble. At first a few of them asked questions and disagreed with Paul about his answers. As time went on so many Jews refused to listen any longer that Paul decided to leave the synagogue and go somewhere else to preach. He rented a hall near the center of the city. Anyone who chose to come was welcome.

Late one afternoon Paul sent Priscilla back to the shop with a message for Aquila. "Paul wanted me to tell you about some strange things that happened in the city today," she reported.

"What is it?" asked Aquila. "Is there some new plot to make trouble for Paul?"

"No! No!" said Priscilla. "The people are burning books. Let me get my breath and I'll tell you about it."

"Books!" exclaimed Aquila. "What kind of books? Who's burning them?"

"It's those magicians," said his wife, "the ones who think they can help people by using magic cures. Paul has been telling them that God's love is stronger than all their magic tricks. More and more of them have been coming to the hall to hear Paul preach about God's power. Well, today in the city square a whole crowd of them brought all their books telling how to make magic charms and spells and such things. They piled the books up in a big heap and set fire to the whole lot. They say they don't believe in magic any more. They believe in Jesus."

"That's great! Bet it made quite a blaze!" exclaimed Aquila. "What did other people say when they saw it?"

"Someone said the books were worth at least fifty thousand pieces of silver," she answered. "Everyone wanted to know why the magicians did it. The men said that they could help others only through the power of Jesus. They're saying there is no other name except that of Jesus by which anyone can live."

"Praise be to God," said Aquila. "Everyone in Ephesus will hear about this. I only hope it will not stir up Paul's enemies again. I don't know what we'd do without Paul."

Paul was able to keep on working, and the church was growing fast. One day friends from Corinth came to visit him. They brought bad news. "You taught us that we are free from the law when we believe in Jesus," they said. "Now many of our people are saying this means that they are free to do anything they like. If we tell them the way they act is wrong, they say they're following your teaching about being free men."

"But I wrote a long letter explaining all that," said Paul. "They *are* free to live in Jesus' way of love, *not* free to do what is harmful. That's what I preached."

"We know that," remarked one of the men, "and we believe you. But people in the church in Corinth are quarreling over whether yours are the only teachings we should follow."

"Our service of worship is a mix-up, too," complained another of the visitors. "Sometimes so many people are talking at once you can't understand what anyone is saying."

Paul looked very sad. "You know how much I love all the people in your church. Many of them are poor and weak, and some are foolish. But I love you all. I will write another letter and try to be more helpful than I was before."

The men carried Paul's letter back with them to Corinth. They read his words to the people. "Paul says that our faith comes from God's power alone. He says that all those who teach us are servants of God. Only Christ can have first place." But many refused to pay any attention to his advice. Some of the people grumbled about Paul's interference.

"Paul says he would be willing to give up anything that might keep others from believing in Jesus," said some of the church people in Corinth. "But we won't give up any of our rights. We know what's wrong and what's right. Others ought to see things our way."

A few faithful followers tried to explain Paul's words. "We must do everything in a spirit of love, for nothing will last unless it is done because of love for others. Only love will never come to an end."

Paul was in Ephesus waiting impatiently for news from Corinth. Would the people there understand his letter? Would they change their ways? Would they try to live in Jesus' way of love instead of quarreling with each other?

Finally word came to Paul that the church people in Corinth refused to pay any attention to what he wrote. "I will go to visit them myself," said Paul. "Surely they will listen to me and change their ways."

But when Paul arrived in Corinth, the people chased him away. They did not want to hear what he had to tell them about Jesus' way of love. They wanted to do things in their own way.

Paul returned to Ephesus. But he would not give up trying to show the people in Corinth the truth about Jesus Christ. He decided to write another very stern letter. "I warned you before," Paul wrote, "and now I am warning you again. If you do not change your ways, I'll come back again to Corinth. And when I come, I will punish those who are causing all this trouble."

One day, while Paul was waiting for a reply, there was a

noisy riot in Ephesus. The silversmiths tried to mob the Christians, and Paul knew that he was the cause of the trouble. "That fellow Paul says that gods made by men's hands are not gods at all," he heard the workmen complain. "Many people believe him, and now they will not buy our statues. Paul is ruining our business with his talk," grumbled the silversmiths.

"I have been in Ephesus for a long time," said Paul to his

friends. "I know our enemies won't stop until they kill me. It seems best for me to leave Ephesus now, and go somewhere else to preach."

Paul started out, hoping to get word from the people in Corinth somewhere along the way. One day a messenger caught up with him. "I bring good news from Corinth, Paul. The ringleaders there have been punished for stirring up the trouble. The people beg you to forgive them. They are truly sorry for all their quarreling."

Paul was overjoyed. At once he dictated a letter of thanksgiving, love, and forgiveness. "You have cleared yourselves of all blame," he wrote. "I give thanks to God that all men will see you are faithful followers of Christ. They may even come to know him through you.

"While I was waiting to hear from you, there was a great deal of trouble and my life was in danger. But I am not afraid—for death would be like walking out of a tent and going off to be with Jesus forever. Our aim is to please him, no matter what happens to us."

Paul came to the end of his letter. "And now, my friends, good-bye. Remember my advice and do not quarrel among yourselves anymore. The God of love and peace be with you."

At last Paul could stop worrying about his beloved friends in Corinth. He was free to go on with his work. "Someday I want to go to Rome," he thought. "But the next thing I must do is to deliver the money that I've been collecting for the poor people in the church in Jerusalem. The gift will show how much their Gentile brothers care about them. Truly we are all one in Christ."

14
To Rome—In Chains

It was festival time in Jerusalem when Paul arrived. The city was full of Jews who had come to worship in the temple. As Paul pushed his way through the crowds, he stopped for a moment to look at the golden dome shining in the sunlight.

"How often men have come here to praise God, only to be driven out by their enemies," Paul said to himself. "There was Jesus, and Stephen . . ." Paul shuddered as he remembered how he had persecuted those who were now his friends in Christ.

Paul walked on toward the house where the elders of the church were waiting. "Will they accept me, and all those faithful believers in the young churches where I preached only the true gospel of Christ?" Paul wondered. "Can we at last really be one church?"

The elders greeted Paul. "Welcome back to Jerusalem, brother Paul. Tell us about your travels. Have you had any success in preaching Jesus Christ?"

Paul told about his work among the Jews and non-Jews alike. The men listened carefully. When he reported the number of faithful followers who had become part of the church, some of the elders shook their heads. Others rocked back and forth in their seats when Paul told them how he had been driven out of the synagogues by the Jews.

Finally one of the elders spoke. "All this is to God's glory, brother Paul. God's power has also been at work here in Jerusalem while you were gone. Thousands of Jews have joined with us, and the church is strong. However, I must remind you that we here think it is very important to keep all the laws of Moses. You have been telling those who live among the Gentiles that they don't need to obey those laws. This may lead to serious trouble when the news gets about that you are here among us."

"I will do anything I can to show that I keep the laws just as carefully as you do," said Paul. "If you have a plan, tell me. The church must not be divided by any acts of ours."

A few days later, before Paul could prove his loyalty, some of his enemies found him praying in the temple. "Men of Israel! Come and help!" they cried out. "Here is that man who has been preaching against us and the Law. He has even dared to bring Gentiles who do not belong here into the most holy part of our temple."

People came running from everywhere. They grabbed Paul, dragged him into the courtyard, and began to beat him. "Kill him!" they shouted. "Kill the one who breaks the law. Get rid of him once and for all!"

The mob became so angry that the Roman guard on duty nearby ran to the barracks for help. "It's those Jews again," he reported. "They are after some poor fellow. I don't know what he's done. Come quickly or they will kill him for sure!"

As soon as the soldiers arrived, the crowd stopped beating Paul. But they kept on shouting, "Kill him! Kill him!"

"We'll never find out who he is or what he has done in all this uproar," yelled the commander. "Take him back to the barracks where we can question him. Pick him up and carry him if you have to. This mob won't let him get away from them without a fight."

Just as Paul was about to be taken into the barracks, he spoke to the commander. "I am a Jew, from the city of Tarsus. May I have your permission to speak to these people?"

The commander nodded his head. The man certainly did not act like an ordinary criminal. Why would he want to speak to a mob that had almost killed him?

"Brothers and fathers, listen while I defend myself," began Paul. "I am a Jew like yourselves. It was here in Jerusalem that I learned the law from the great Gamaliel. It was here that I tried to show my love for God by persecuting the followers of Jesus."

The mob was quieter now. Perhaps they had been wrong about this man. They listened carefully as Paul told the story of how his life had been completely changed after Jesus spoke to him that day long ago on the Damascus road.

"I returned to Jerusalem," he continued, "after I knew that God had chosen me to be his witness. I did not want to leave the city then. I wanted to stay and tell all the followers of Jesus that I had become a believer, too. But as I stood praying in the temple one day, I again heard Jesus speaking to me. He told me to get out of Jerusalem without delay. He said that the people would not accept what I had to tell them. Jesus said to me, 'Go, for I am sending you far away to preach to the Gentiles.' "

At those words, Paul heard the crowd begin to roar and shout. "Take him away. He's not fit to live on this earth!"

The commander had heard enough. "Get him inside," he commanded. "Find out what he has done to make these Jews so angry. Beat him if he won't talk, but find out what this riot is all about."

Inside the barracks the soldiers began to tie Paul to the whipping post. "Wait a minute!" he demanded. "Is it lawful for you to whip a Roman citizen? Especially one who has not been found guilty of any crime?"

"You're a Roman citizen?" asked the commander. "It cost me a lot of money to become a citizen. What price did you pay?"

"I was born a citizen," answered Paul.

The commander became frightened. It was against the law to whip a Roman citizen. "Set the prisoner free at once," he ordered. "But keep him here where he is safe from that mob outside. Tomorrow I shall order a trial to be held. Then maybe we can get to the bottom of all this trouble."

Paul knew very well that the Jews did not care about giving him a fair trial. The next morning, as soon as the com-

To Rome—In Chains

mander brought him before the temple leaders, another fight started. Once again the soldiers had to take Paul back to the barracks to save him from being beaten to death.

In the meantime, Paul's friends, who found out about a plot to kill him, sent Paul's young nephew to tell him. Paul immediately asked a guard to let his nephew speak with the commander. "The prisoner Paul is my uncle," the young man explained. "We have learned that the temple leaders are going to ask you to bring him before them again tomorrow. When you do, more than forty men will be hiding and waiting to capture Paul. They have sworn not to eat or drink anything until they've killed him!"

"Do not tell anyone that you came to see me," said the commander. "I'll find a way to get your uncle safely out of Jerusalem. Go home, now, and don't tell anyone else about this."

That night a soldier opened the door of Paul's cell. "Follow me," he said. Very quietly Paul followed the soldier outside where a horse was waiting to take him to another city. He looked around in surprise, for the commander had ordered seventy horsemen and a great squad of soldiers to protect Paul on the journey. "This may get me a little closer to Rome," thought Paul as they started off in the darkness. "I know that I am to speak there someday in the name of Jesus."

Soon Paul would find that there was more trouble ahead. The armed guard had orders to take him to the Roman governor. He would hear the case and decide what to do with the prisoner. Some Jews came down from Jerusalem and wanted to tell their side of the story. "I will decide this case later," said the governor. "We'll keep Paul here as our prisoner. His friends may visit him, however, and do for him whatever he wishes."

Two years went by, and Paul was still waiting for his case to be settled. In the meantime, a new governor was appointed. Once again Paul's enemies in Jerusalem were plotting how to kill him. "Have him sent back to Jerusalem," they said. "We can more easily prove our charges against him here."

"Are you willing to go to Jerusalem and stand trial before me there?" the new governor asked Paul. He wanted very much to keep on the good side of the Jews.

But Paul refused to be tricked. He knew his rights. He also saw a chance to get to Rome. "I've committed no wrong against the Jewish Law, nor the temple, nor the Roman Emperor," he said. "I am standing here before the Roman court. For two years I have been a prisoner. Why should I go back to Jerusalem now to be tried? If I have done anything wrong against Rome, you can punish me. You know well enough that I have done no wrong to the Jews, so you have no right to send me back to them. I am a Roman citizen, and I ask to be heard by Caesar himself in Rome."

There was nothing more the governor could do. Paul had the right as a Roman citizen to be heard by the Emperor. To the Emperor he would have to go.

When sailing time came, Paul boarded the ship along with several other prisoners. Things went well until the passengers changed to another boat that was to take them on to Rome. The wind was against them and the going was slow. "It will soon be winter," said the captain. "We must go on a little farther and find a harbor where we can be safe from the storms."

Paul tried to tell them that it was dangerous to try to go on, but no one would listen. Before long a great storm blew the ship about so badly that the crew was not able to do anything but lower the mainsail and let her float. Even when they threw the cargo overboard, it didn't seem to help.

Day after day the storm raged. Food was scarce and the men grew weak from working too hard without rest. "You should have listened to me," said Paul. "If we'd stayed where we were, all this trouble wouldn't have happened to us. But do not lose your courage. God has let me know that not one of us will lose his life. Only the ship will be lost. We'll be cast ashore somewhere on an island."

Two weeks passed and the ship was still drifting in the sea. One night the sailors thought they could hear a sound like waves breaking on the shore. "Land must be near, but it's too dark to see for sure!" a crewman called.

Just before daybreak, Paul told everyone to eat some food to gain strength. "Remember, not one of you will be hurt," he assured them. Then he gave thanks to God for the bread, and everyone ate. As the sun rose, the men could see the sandy shore of an island just ahead.

"Cast off the anchors! Free the rudder. Set the foresail to the wind. We'll make a run for the beach!" Paul heard the captain shout. Before the crew had time to obey, the ship struck a sandbank and couldn't move.

"We're being pounded to pieces by the waves!" cried the captain. "Every man who can swim, jump over the side. Everyone else find a piece of plank or something else to hold onto. The waves will carry you to shore."

Paul and all the men got safely to land, just as he had claimed. For three months they lived on the island. During this time Paul preached to those willing to listen. He healed many who were sick and made a great number of good friends among the people there.

Finally one day the captain said, "Winter is over and there is no longer any danger from storms. A ship will be ready to leave in a few days. They have room for all of us, so be ready to sail."

Once again Paul stood on the deck of a ship saying goodbye to friends. "Peace be to you. And many thanks for the gifts you've given us. We will remember you always in our prayers."

This time the journey was a quiet one. When the ship docked, Paul and the other prisoners started on foot down the road leading to the great city of Rome. Along the way groups of Christians from Rome came out to greet Paul. It was good to be able to meet some of the people to whom he had written so long ago.

"Where am I to go when we reach Rome?" Paul asked the commander. "Will I have to stay in prison until my trial?"

"You may live wherever you wish," replied the commander, "but I must leave a guard with you day and night. Your friends may come to see you, but you are not free to go about the city."

What a strange way for Paul to be visiting the city he had wanted to visit for so long. Almost the first thing he did was to send for the Jewish leaders in Rome. "My brothers, I am a prisoner here, even though I have done nothing against our people or the Jewish laws or the temple. I want you to know that I'm not guilty of any crime. I wear these chains for the sake of Jesus who is your Messiah and mine."

"We have not had letters from Jerusalem telling us about your coming," they said. "But we'll listen to your ideas. No one here has anything good to say about the Christians."

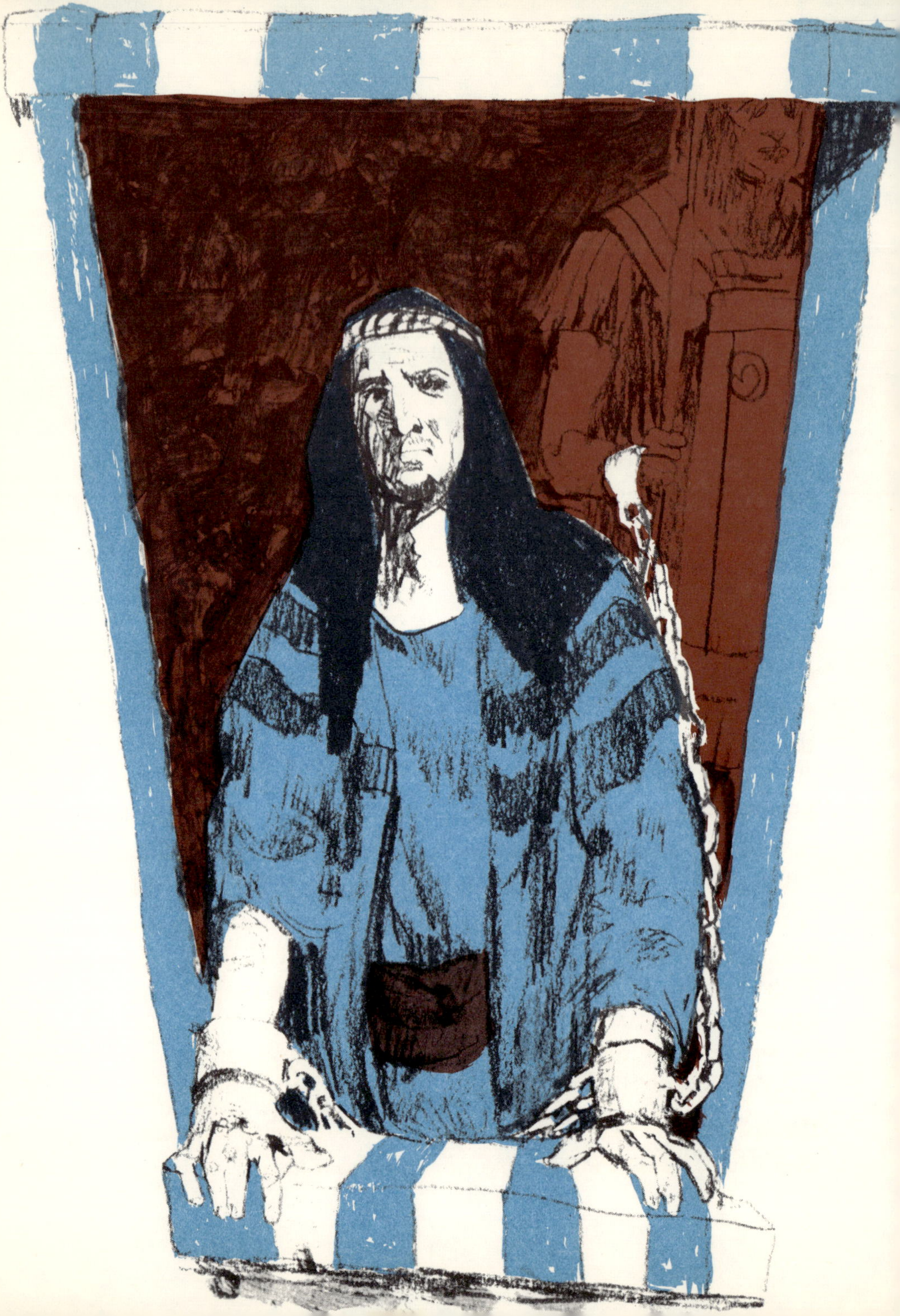

To Rome—In Chains

Many people came to hear Paul and to talk with him. From early morning till night he preached about Jesus, but not everyone believed what he said. Often Paul remembered what the prophets had said long ago: "Some will listen but not understand. Some will look but not see anything."

Two years went by, and still Paul was waiting for his trial to take place. Whenever he could, Paul taught those who came that God wants men to find a new life of love in Jesus Christ. Visitors from churches where he had once preached came to see Paul and ask for his advice. Sometimes they brought news of friends, and sometimes they brought gifts and messages of love.

Paul wrote many letters explaining that all men everywhere are welcome in the fellowship of faith and love that is Christ's church. He wanted everyone to know that nothing would ever be able to defeat God's way of love for those who believe in Jesus as Lord.

Sometimes Paul would stand by his window and look out into the street where he was not allowed to go. The chains that bound him to his soldier guard clanked when he moved. "What will come of all this?" he wondered. "If I live, I will live for Christ. That will be good. If I die, that would be good also. I could leave all this trouble and go to be with the Lord. I am glad Jesus gave his life for me, and I am glad to suffer for him now.

"I know what it's like to be poor and a prisoner. I know what it is to have plenty of all that I need. I know all about the ups and downs of life. God will give me strength for whatever comes," said Paul to anyone who pitied him.

Day after day Paul watched the soldiers standing their guard while the visitors came and went. He gave thanks for the friends who cared for his needs. Paul was not afraid of the enemies who hatched their plots to kill him. He was a prisoner in Rome, but Paul still was Christ's own man. Nothing could ever again separate him from God.

"Praise be to God who gives us this victory . . ." was the song that Paul would always sing.

Scripture References

You may want to read parts of this story as it is told in the Bible. Here is a list of references that will tell you where to look for some of the main incidents in this book.

Chapter 1 —Deut. 6: 4–5 for the words of the Shema, which Paul probably learned as soon as he was able to speak.
—Acts 22; Phil. 3: 5; Acts 18: 3 for references to events in Saul's youth.
Chapter 2 —Acts 22: 3 and references for Chapter 1.
Chapter 3 —Rom. 7: 24; Gal. 1: 14; Acts 3—4.
Chapter 4 —Acts 4—8.
Chapter 5 —Acts 9: 1–19; Acts 26: 9–18; Acts 22: 3–21.
Chapter 6 —Acts 9: 20–31; Acts 22: 17–21.
Chapter 7 —Acts 10: 9—11: 18; Acts 11: 19–30; Acts 13: 1–12.
Chapter 8 —Acts 13: 13–52.
Chapter 9 —Acts 14: 6–20.
Chapter 10—Acts 14: 21—15: 35.
Chapter 11—Acts 15: 36—16: 40.
Chapter 12—Acts 18: 1–21.
Chapter 13—Acts 19: 1—20: 1; 1 Cor. 1: 1–17; 3: 1–9; 1 Cor. 16: 8–9; 2 Cor. 2: 1–3; 1 Cor. 13.
Chapter 14—Acts 21—28.

Mrs. Priester who wrote this book for you spends the winter in Chicago, Illinois. She lives there with her husband, who teaches in a seminary, and their son David. In the summertime the Priesters head for a quiet, restful farmhouse in Peacham, Vermont.

Mrs. Priester started thinking about Paul and writing this book one cold winter in Illinois. When June came she, Dr. Priester, and David packed all her books and papers into the back of their station wagon and started out for a summer in the Green Mountains of Vermont. The books and papers were almost lost when their station wagon caught fire one day. A truck driver stopped with a fire extinguisher which didn't work! Finally a patrolman came with one that did. He and the truck driver helped the Priesters save their belongings. So Mrs. Priester was able to continue her work on your book.

Late one night as Mrs. Priester put the final touches on your book, she wrote these words: "Just now I have no more thoughts about Paul. I like him very much. This pondering with him has taught me more than I expected to learn about forgiveness through faith."

Shannon Stirnweis, who illustrated this book, was born in Portland, Oregon. He studied painting at the University of Oregon and was graduated with distinction from the Art Center School in Los Angeles. During his army days, he served for sixteen months as an illustrator in Germany.

He has illustrated another CLC book, *God and His Covenant People*.

Mr. Stirnweis now lives in New York with his wife, Regina, and his two sons, Kevin and Kirk.